The
LASKETT
Herefordshire
Created by
SIR ROY STRONG
&
DR JULIA TREVELYAN OMAN

ROY STRONG

THE LASKETT

THE STORY OF A GARDEN

BANTAM PRESS

LONDON · NEW YORK · TORONTO · SYDNEY · AUCKLAND

TRANSWORLD PUBLISHERS
61–63 Uxbridge Road, London W5 5SA
a division of The Random House Group Ltd

RANDOM HOUSE AUSTRALIA (PTY) LTD
20 Alfred Street, Milsons Point, Sydney,
New South Wales 2061, Australia

RANDOM HOUSE NEW ZEALAND LTD
18 Poland Road, Glenfield, Auckland 10, New Zealand

RANDOM HOUSE SOUTH AFRICA (PTY) LTD
Endulini, 5a Jubilee Road, Parktown 2193, South Africa

Published 2003 by Bantam Press
a division of Transworld Publishers

A catalogue record for this book is available from the British Library.
ISBN 0593 050703

Printed by Appl Druck, Wemding, Germany

1 3 5 7 9 10 8 6 4 2

Now thank we all our God

CONTENTS

PREFACE

I AM NOT SURE HOW TO INTRODUCE THIS BOOK. IT IS ONE WHICH HAD TO be written, or rather which I felt within myself that I had to write, even it if was to remain unpublished. I have read a number of books by people who have made gardens, but somehow what you will read here doesn't quite fit into that category. Indeed, I can't think where it fits. I suppose if I had to place it within the orbit of my own writing I would site it somewhere between the *Diaries* and *A Country Life*. It is in a sense a horticultural autobiography, the life of a man who, suddenly at thirty-eight, was entranced by gardens. And not only for the horticultural delight they offered him but perhaps even more for the deeper resonance they could express about human relationships and aspirations and life. One person in a sense lives many lives. In my own case there has been the life of scholarship, amply charted in the steady stream of books over four decades; another is one's public life, recorded in the diaries of my years as director of two of our greatest art institutions. The latter catch something of the mask and the face, for the making of The Laskett garden always figures in them as an inner joy, one of the deepest and most creative expressions of the private man. *The Laskett* is, in a sense, a fuller exploration of that territory. Those familiar with the verses of the hymn of which the first line only is etched onto the dedication page will know precisely what this book is about.

ROY STRONG, THE LASKETT

THE ELOPEMENT

O N 10 SEPTEMBER 1971 I ELOPED AND MARRIED JULIA TREVELYAN OMAN IN the church of Wilmcote, Shakespeare's mother Mary Arden's village, just outside Stratford-upon-Avon. Why elope? I was thirty-five and Julia was forty. Both of us felt passionately that marriage was a deeply personal and private affair, a sacrament, not to be sullied by the hurly burly of a public wedding. Neither of us would have done it in any other way. Thirty years on, the romance of that elopement is as vivid to me as on the day.

This may seem a strange point of departure for a book about the creation of a garden, except, but for that event, there would have been none. Not that the making of a great garden together had even flickered across my mind at that juncture, although I was even then acutely conscious that the world of plants meant much to Julia. I knew that somehow our wedding breakfast table had to have at its centre at the very least some sprays of rosemary (she had already given me one) and, above all, honeysuckle. Why rosemary and why honeysuckle, you may ask. Both are old-fashioned English plants, one a herb, the other a flower; both had flourished in the gardens of Shakespeare's England. They also shared the beguiling attribute of scent. It was, indeed, working together on a little book on my heroine, Elizabeth I, which had been the prelude to my proposal. Honeysuckle stood for great Gloriana, for in her portraits her dresses could be embroidered with its spiralling leaves and flowers, and in one she actually holds a sprig of it in her hand. This was a marriage brought about by the Virgin Queen.

And what of the rosemary? A branch of rosemary was always to have resonance for Julia and this is the reason. Her mother, Joan, one of the eight children of Sir Ernest Trevelyan, had lost her mother when she was just one. Although Sir Ernest was quickly to marry again, in a sense the children remained tragic souls, orphans, but for one person, a nanny whose nickname was Dooks. She gave her whole life and love to raising the Trevelyan children in a rambling late Victorian house in north Oxford. That giving is summed up in the fact that at some stage she had married, but neither Sir

PREVIOUS PAGE *Orchard vista*
OPPOSITE PAGE *Bride and groom*

Ernest, nor their stepmother, nor they, ever knew, until one day by accident Dooks forgot to take off her wedding ring, and then it could no longer be concealed. They loved and cherished Dooks to the day she died, and it was from her that the great bushy, coarse *Rosmarinus officinalis* at Putney, Julia's parents' home, came. Understandably its status was iconic, caught supremely on the day of my mother-in-law's funeral, when Julia went into the garden, pulled off a huge billowing branch and laid it as the solitary floral tribute on her mother's coffin. Its descendants were to thrive and multiply in the garden that I did not guess then we were to create together.

It was one thing to know that the presence of these plants was to mean so much to Julia. It was quite another to get them. In this I had the good fortune to have as my best man David Hutt, a keen gardener, now a canon of Westminster Abbey but then a curate attached to the priest who married us, the eccentric and lovable Gerard Irvine. It was David who secured a branch of rosemary and who searched the hedgerows for a last lingering sprig of wild honeysuckle and saw that the required flowers were in the middle of the table at our wedding breakfast.

That I proposed to Julia at all had a plant context. On the day before I did, I happened to be talking at a party to Lindy Dufferin – the painter Lindy Guinness – saying how I adored Julia, and Lindy, in her role as matchmaker, said, 'Grab her, whatever happens, she is there as happiness and home, loving and caring for each other, watching the plants grow together.' The next day, 20 July, I popped the question, appropriately in St James's Park. Almost three decades later I found myself sitting next to Lindy at a lunch given in the grounds of Croome Park, the great landscape masterpiece by 'Capability' Brown. The gathering was in memory of someone else who will figure in this narrative, the late George Clive, whose memorial is a contribution to this garden's restoration by the National Trust. Sitting at a trestle table in a dilapidated farm shed, I reminded Lindy of her perceptive matchmaking all those years ago, which she had quite forgotten. Looking back, it was her description of marriage being about planting a flower together – nurturing it, watching it grow and then blossom – which stuck in my mind, and still does today.

Everything was in place for the wedding to happen on the morning after the first night of Julia's production of *Othello* for the Royal Shakespeare Company at Stratford. Julia's profession is that of a designer, by that date a distinguished one with credits such as Jonathan Miller's *Alice* and Tony Richardson's *The Charge of the Light Brigade* to her name. I was still the young and somewhat dashing director of the National Portrait Gallery. One small detail of our marriage service was also a presage of what was to come. It opened with an exchange of gifts, which Gerard wished to bless by sprinkling them with holy water. But, alas, the tiny dog-kennel of a church was bereft of stoop and sprinkler, so a branch of dark green yew was plucked from one of the ancient trees in the churchyard. Little did I know then that so much of the coming decades was to be taken up with the nurturing, training and clipping of that most magisterially English of all garden plants.

Although I was wholly unconscious of it, much was already in place indicating that a garden of some kind was to be part of the scheme of things. But a garden calls for space and when I married all I could offer was the tiny paved courtyard garden of a small Gothick town house in Brighton. Moreover, marriage calls for making a home together. And so it was that in the spring of 1972 we began the search that was eventually to lead us to The Laskett.

BELOW *Nymph and shepherd: Cecil Beaton's photograph a few days after the wedding*

One

THE INHERITANCE

WHY DID WE WISH TO LIVE IN THE COUNTRY, THE READER MIGHT ASK. After all, I had been born a Londoner and my work was London-based. Julia had been born and had lived in London also, and her work, too, was London-based. I think I can best answer by quoting from a letter I wrote to my Dutch friend Jan van Dorsten, shortly after we moved in May 1973: 'London is such HELL these days – the gas is on strike, the hospitals, the Civil Service, the railways. It's a bad period for people in these islands, full of deep unrest.' We had made up our minds already, after marrying, that we would buy the house where we would ultimately end our days, but the decision that that should be sited away from London was sharpened by the climate of the times. I recall that we sat one weekend in my pretty house in Brighton devoid of heating and unable to cook as the electric companies were on strike. Even the traffic lights didn't work. An urban environment we saw as vulnerable. The seventies was one prolonged period of dislocation and turbulence. At least, we thought, with a house in the country we could grow our own food and burn our own wood. In addition, we longed for privacy, for a space away from the perpetual glitz and glitter of what in retrospect one can see as the dying throes of the swinging sixties extravaganza.

The early seventies was an unpropitious time for house-hunting and we had little money, but we began by drawing up some kind of specification of what we sought, a document which now reads as appallingly naive and optimistic: 'Type: small manor house, rectory or gentleman's house', ending with the sentence: 'We are not interested in land basically but want a maintainable garden.' Not much sign of *furor hortensis* there as yet. This specification was then distributed hopefully to various estate agents.

Our initial foray was in the Oxfordshire area, for Julia had spent much of her war-time childhood in Oxford in Frewin Hall, a rambling old house with extensive grounds surprisingly tucked away in the middle of the city. It had been leased to her grandfather, Sir Charles Oman, Chichele Professor of Modern History and Fellow of All Souls, from Brasenose College. So Oxford it was to be, and though in the end that was not to happen, both Oxford and the Omans were to become etched into the garden story.

The idea of a house in that area of the country was to linger in the background throughout the search, and we saw many, but we were outpriced. Ludicrous price tags were attached to what were little more than decrepit cottages. Failure to purchase half of a splendid seventeenth-century house in Northamptonshire left a tearful Julia and me determined to take some kind of immediate action. It so chanced that I mentioned our woes to a friend who promptly said that there was a rectory listed for sale that day in the property section of *The Times* at Bishop's Frome in Herefordshire. It was to go to auction on 20 September and was billed in *Country Life* as follows: 'A substantial village residence offering considerable scope for improvement.' A photograph showed an extensive brick-built Victorian house with commodious windows overlooking an expanse of lawn.

So it was that we left London early the next morning for Herefordshire. It was not a county I knew, apart from a brief visit with a friend when I was an undergraduate, perched on the back of his motorcycle, visiting remote churches. It was, however, far more familiar to Julia. Her parents had had friends, the Gardners, who had inherited the estate attached to Yatton Court in the north of the county, a beautiful Georgian house bordered on one side by the waters of the River Lugg, with a yew walk whose mysterious beauty had cast its spell on her when, as a teenager, she had stayed there. But, as we were to learn, north and south Herefordshire are two different worlds, cut asunder by the hill topped by Queenswood north of Hereford itself. Those in the north look northwards to Shropshire and Cheshire, those in the south to Gloucester, Cheltenham and the Malverns. Our destiny was to be in the south, and Bishop's Frome lay close to Worcestershire.

I'll never forget that first drive west. There's an extraordinary moment after Gloucester when the land suddenly rises just past Highnam (seat of Thomas Gambier Parry, the great art collector, and later, I was to find, gardener) and winds and twists its way up and over, by way of Weston-under-Penyard, to the hilltop town of Ross-on-Wye. Suddenly I was aware that I was entering the landscape of the Picturesque, that part of the country celebrated at the close of the eighteenth century by the likes of William Sawrey Gilpin and Sir Uvedale Price. Its beauty resides in its asymmetry, its dramatic changes of level and rich afforestation, its ruined abbeys and castles, as well as the modest, huddled houses and farms scattered along its sinuous silvery waters, above all the River Wye. Each twist and turn of the road brought another vista, another view whose beauty was framed by the branches of ancient trees. Later I was to discover that Downton Castle,

Richard Payne Knight's legendary garden, fount of the Picturesque, was in Herefordshire, and, not so far away from where we were to live, was the Repton landscape of Garnons, at that time being restored by the peppery Sir Richard Cotterell.

We made the drive on one of those golden autumn days effulgent with Keatsian mellow fruitfulness, which, in Herefordshire's case, was expressed in the cider apple orchards that stretched on either side of us as we travelled through the lowland areas. It made everything before that ascent and descent seem like the suburbs. Here, it seemed, was the golden land, remote, beckoning, a place in which to hide and be hidden. But, alas, much to our disappointment, we failed in our bid for Bishop's Frome, in retrospect a blessing for it carried only an acre of land and the cost of restoring the crumbling house would have financially crippled us. Retreating dispirited, we took up an invitation made through the Gardners to the firm of local estate agents, Russell, Baldwin & Bright, for we had reached the decision that it was to Herefordshire that we would come. David Wells, their cheerful representative, faced with the two downhearted newlyweds, said, 'Don't worry. I'll find you a house, if it's the last thing I do.' And he was to be true to his word, sooner than was ever anticipated.

Not long after, the telephone rang and it was David Wells. 'I think I have a house for you,' he said to Julia. 'It belongs to a lady recently widowed who wants to sell it privately. But you must come quickly.' Little did we know that David was in fact choosing his neighbours, for he and his wife still live opposite, a little along the lane.

It was already late October and the leaves had fallen when we first set eyes on what was to be the site of our future garden, the house called The

Laskett. It lay midway between Ross-on-Wye and Hereford, two fields off the A49 along a lane called Laskett Lane. Looking three decades on at the photographs taken during that winter, I am struck above all by the emptiness, almost bleakness, of it all, the house and its surroundings seeming little more than a blank canvas awaiting the artist to wield his brush. But the house was pleasing, reminiscent of a small rectory out of a

The Laskett garden as we found it, winter 1972-73

novel by Jane Austen, rectangular, built of pink sandstone with a steeply pitched tiled roof and tall chimney stacks, at the front three sash windows above, and below two later bay windows, flanking a wooden entrance porch. As Julia remarked it was building, not architecture, rural Regency of an undistinguished kind, but the proportions were good. There were later accretions, a small wing to one side and additions at the back. Behind there was a stable coach house across a narrow yard with a mounting block. And that, apart from the garage and some nondescript sheds, was it.

The garden was tidy but unexceptional. A wide, high thuja hedge lined the drive to one side, obscuring a clear view of the facade of the house, around which stretched lawn at the front and to one side. There was an herbaceous border before it that led on to a gravel path flanked by a rose bed. A mock wellhead was a solitary indication that perhaps once the garden had been more interesting, but now everything had been reduced to an expanse of easy-to-maintain greensward backed by a new shrubbery screening out a view of the farm, Penny Pitt, behind. On the drive side of the house there was a Judas tree planted on an island, around which cars could turn, backed by a larch screen with rambler roses. That led on to the vegetable garden, then a decayed greenhouse and, finally, the garage.

We hardly took in the adjacent two-acre field, still called by us the Field, which, we were told, was let out to a local farmer for his cattle. But, adding that to what we had taken in, the area overall was a fan-shaped tract of land in which the house and garden proper were tucked into the easternmost point. What we did fall in love with on first sight was the mighty cedar of Lebanon that stood proudly at the base of the front lawn. I see it now as I write, its branches bearing fronds of evergreen needles reaching out towards me. To have such a tree is a wonderful bonus for any garden, for it becomes a reference point from every part of the domain. To that could be added a line of Spanish chestnuts up the drive, a magnificent beech to one side of the house and a Turkey oak and ancient yew on its other side, plus a scattering of elms. One more tree had significance, a tall pine at the top of the drive on the left. My father-in-law, Charles

The Laskett framed by branches of the cedar, winter 1972-73

19

Oman, the distinguished authority on silver and former Keeper of Metalwork at the Victoria & Albert Museum, on first seeing it remarked, 'Ah, a Charlie tree,' meaning that The Laskett was a safe house for Jacobites, for tradition has it that such trees were planted as covert signals to the Young Pretender that here he would find welcome and shelter.

The house itself was south-facing, sited on a gentle gradient. Westwards the view was to the Black Mountains, gaunt barren hills seemingly either holding the Welsh in or keeping the English out, certainly firmly reminding us, as the place names did, that this was oft-fought-over border country. Soon we were to learn to dread the west wind pounding both house and garden. Looking south-west from the front of the house the view was of rolling farmland with fields full of the prize Herefordshire cattle of our neighbours, the Symonds of Llandinabo Court. In the distance was May Hill, topped by a circle of pine trees. For years when we drove down we would spot May Hill from afar signalling that home was on its other side.

I need hardly add that the decision to purchase was immediate. The house was to be ours on May Day 1973. Millie Bryant, the vendor, wrote to us on 24 October saying, 'I do so hope you will find happiness and peace here,' ending, 'That's Rosemary for remembrance,' enclosing a sprig from The Laskett garden. Today that sprig is mounted in our scrapbooks alongside the photographs of the house as we found it. From Millie we learnt a little of its history, in particular that Sir Edward Elgar had visited The Laskett, apparently pinching the maids. Be that as it may, Elgar's presence only served to make everything seem even righter, for one of Julia's greatest triumphs had been the ballet *Enigma Variations* danced to his haunting music, her concept but choreographed by Sir Frederick Ashton for the Royal Ballet in 1968. Everything was in place for the great day when we would move in, which was fixed for 3 May 1973.

WHAT DOES THE WORD 'LASKETT' MEAN? APPARENTLY IT IS HEREFORDSHIRE dialect for a strip of land 'without' the parish, as the historic term goes. That accords with the dictionary definition: 'lasket (or latchet), one of the loops or rings of cord by which a bonnet is attached to the foot of a sail; alternately, latchet, a loop; *a narrow strip of anything*, a thong.' The Laskett is literally a strip of land outside the main confines of the parish of Llanwarne. Another explanation is that it derives from 'glas-coed' or greensward, but even that is uncertain. Early Ordnance Survey maps record a Laskett Wood or Grove further along the lane on the south side.

The three acres in which the house stands were once part of the Blewhenstone estate and were sold by Sir Edwyn Francis Scudamore to one Joseph Ashbarry on 12 November 1839, when they were in the tenure or occupancy of Charles Meadmore. No mention is made of a house, but barely six weeks later Ashbarry sold them on to William Matthews. In this document the house for the first time appears: 'all that messuage or dwellinghouse and all other Erections and Buildings lately erected and built and standing...' The vital word is 'lately', indicating that the house must be late 1830s, that is, early Victorian in date. The earliest Ordnance Survey maps from the 1830s show no sign of the house, which first appears on the 1840 Tithe Award Map. Mention should also be made at this point of the very narrow strip of land along Laskett Lane also recorded on that map, on which stood what was then called Cross Collar Cottage. That, by the time we arrived, had become Laskett Cottage, and was eventually to be incorporated into our garden as The Folly. The map also provides field names; in the case of our field, it was called 'The Two Acres'.

The Matthews family were timber merchants who owned what was to become Whitewells House opposite, close to Cross Collar. The land in that area must then have been wooded, for what fortune they made came from supplying timber for ships during the Napoleonic Wars. The Laskett passed from William Matthews (1804–1863) to his third son, Thomas (1848–1929), a chemist and JP of Ross-on-Wye. None of the Matthews family seems ever to have lived here. The house began quite humbly as Laskett Cottage but, by 1900, was known as The Laskett and was let out to a succession of tenants. The earliest was a cleric, the Rev. Rowland Hill, who was in residence in 1840. From 1900 onwards the occupancy is clear and a contract of 1905 letting it to Henry Hogarth Bracewell contains the earliest references to a greenhouse, a conservatory, a stable coach house, the three acres of meadow or pasture and 'the lawn garden'.

In 1922 Thomas Matthews sold it to George William Wilkes, described as 'gentleman', and in that deed we learn further about the grounds in the phrase 'with the Gardens Pleasure Grounds and Lands and appurtances ... Together with the Greenhouse Stable Coachhouse and other buildings and meadow or pastureland'. Poor greenhouse! It was still standing when we arrived, albeit decrepit. We asked the builders for an estimate to repair it but by the time that was produced it had blown down. From Wilkes The Laskett passed, in 1934, to a hunting widow, Edith Wreford Brown. She modestly extended the domain by purchasing a rectangle of land, now our kitchen garden, from the Paines of Penny Pitt, for kennels for the hounds.

Mrs Wreford Brown appeared to live here in a degree of style and I only wish we knew more about her. Laskett Lodge, as it is now called but then was Withy Brae, erected directly opposite what became The Folly, was built by her for her chauffeur and general handyman, Jack Bevan, who lived there with his wife long after we arrived. They were rubicund, kindly people (it was whispered that she had once been in royal service), who kept an eye on The Laskett and fed our cats during all those years when we had to be in London. To extract any information about the house in its Wreford Brown days was agony. Jack would begin only to be halted in his tracks by his wife who would say, 'Now, Jack ...' He did, however, produce photographs showing that once the windows had been shuttered, and he did also, more tantalizingly, describe the garden on the far side of the house, where the well was sited, as being 'like the pages in a book'. What this exactly meant I have never discovered, but something substantial must once have been there, judging by the barrowloads of rock carried away from that site whenever one dug deeper than a foot. It was Jack Bevan who 'designed' the extension to one side of the house to accommodate the cook-housekeeper, and at the same period it was extended at the rear to incorporate a bathroom, scullery, back stairs and stable maid's bedroom. To Mrs Wreford Brown we owe the garage with its observation pit, the thuja hedge up the drive and a rectangular pond which, we were told, was constructed on the outbreak of war in 1939 to house water to be used in case the house was bombed!

Mrs Wreford Brown died in 1946 and the house passed to Colonel and Mrs Jenny. Its great days were over and one senses a steady downhill descent in the new servantless age. From the Jennys it fell into the hands of developers and from them it passed to Colonel and Mrs Bryant and thence to us. From the moment the transaction was made I was enchanted by the place, although Julia pointed out its lack of a large room and how, ever since marrying me, she had come to live in smaller and smaller houses. In my case the reverse was true. But in the years to come all of that was to be remedied. So the scene is set, but what were our gardening credentials?

Mine could never be described as other than thin. Anything to do with the garden and gardening during my childhood was overshadowed by the figure of my father. The garden, to use my mother's words, was 'your father's', a domain untouchable by any other member of the family. George Edward Clement Strong, to give him his full name, was one of life's failures. He should never have married, much less have had children, for he treated my mother like a servant and took no interest whatever in the three boys whom he had sired. But he was, I have to admit, a gardener, in retrospect a saving grace. I have often puzzled as to where this feeling for the earth came from and I would hazard that this redeeming gift came from his mother. Rachel Peake was a strong-willed countrywoman born at South Elmham, near Bungay in Suffolk, in 1864, and one of those countless thousands who drifted to the metropolis in the late Victorian period. She was always to maintain her links with her country origins. It is easy to forget how much that vigorous tradition of modest urban gardening, which was to last until just after the Second World War, owed to that generation. The cottage garden, with its emphasis on self-sufficiency, had not yet become a distant memory. To them it was still a living reality to be transported into the city. So, whenever she visited my parents' house, she always demanded to see the garden. There she would stand and pronounce on the fruiting potential of this or that tree for the year.

Colne Road in Winchmore Hill in North London was part of one of those developments that mushroomed between the wars, adding yet another belt to the ever-widening conurbation of London. It was newly built on what had been orchard land in 1928, the year my parents married, a terrace house with bay windows, a wooden gate opening onto a crazy-paving path flanked by lawn leading to the front door. The front garden itself was held in by the kind of privet hedge that was so fashionable at that period, part of which was trained to form steps and domes and swags. In my teens I was allowed to cut it and it gave me huge pleasure to re-establish its architectural shape. It was my earliest essay in what was to become a passion, topiary.

23 Colne Road

At the rear the garden was the usual long rectangle of London clay with fencing either side topped by trellis, and a wooden garage at the far end. Faded photographs tell me that garden was not devoid of delights. The large rectangle of lawn, necessary with young children, was framed by flower borders rich in herbaceous plants, above all Russell Lupins and feathery cosmos. The straight crazy-paving garden path, which led to the back gate, was straddled by four larchwood arches luxuriantly festooned with climbing roses, and before the garage stood another larchwood screen for climbers. Close to the house there was a Victoria plum tree, along one of the fences two espaliered William's pear trees, and, next to the back gate, a rowan that sported bright orange berries each autumn. Everything was kept in immaculate order.

I don't remember that pre-war garden, for I was just four when war broke out in 1939. My earliest memories are of what replaced it. 'Dig for victory' meant that both front and back gardens were given over to the cultivation of produce. Beneath the bay windows at the front stood rows of neatly staked tomatoes, their fruit-bearing branches trained and tied for support. To hasten their ripening they would sometimes be picked green or on the turn, brought into the house and left to ripen on a warm windowsill. In the back garden the lawn, the rose arches and screen all vanished, giving way to rows of vegetables. I recall potatoes, runner beans, marrows, turnips, spring onions, radishes, cucumbers and lettuce. At the bottom of the garden a chicken run was built, which provided us with eggs through the year and, at Christmas, a roast bird to mark the festival. When the Victoria plum fruited, my mother went into overdrive making jam, and the inevitable glut of green tomatoes was made into chutney. The William's pears would be harvested hard by my father and carefully wrapped, each one in newspaper, and stored in a dark dry place until such time as they ripened. Strangely enough he never planted an apple tree, at times, it seemed, almost deliberately just to annoy my mother. But during these war-time years a heavy crop of produce in any neighbour's garden brought generous gifts. Looking back, I am grateful to have experienced this degree of self-sufficiency. I was to rediscover it again at The Laskett.

Was I never given a packet of Rainbow Mix, the fate of every child? Of course I was. The packet carried a storybook image of a thatched cottage arising from an explosion of sweet-scented stocks, hollyhocks, cornflowers and larkspur. I scattered it on a small patch of earth with impatience. Nothing as far as I can remember germinated. Once I was given a tiny area to cultivate and into it I moved plants such as marigolds in full flower only to find them dead the next day. After the war the garden never regained its pre-1939 glory. A lawn and borders of sorts came back and my father constructed a small pond for goldfish backed by a rockery by which he would sit on warm summer

Garden pioneers, November 1973

We embark on the garden

evenings. In summer the front garden was planted up with antirrhinums grown from seed, the borders edged with the blue and white of alyssum and lobelia typical of the Victorian age. Each summer two hanging baskets were suspended from the projecting front porch, filled with pelargoniums. Their watering every evening was a daily ritual of recrimination as my mother complained of the debris that fell onto the doorstep. Sadly the overall memory left by that thirties suburban garden was that it was part of the division that rent the house in two throughout my childhood. It was never at any time a shared joy.

The reality of gardening was not to impinge on my consciousness again until, in 1969, I purchased a Regency Gothick terrace in Brighton, my first house. This brought with it an apology for a garden, a small walled enclosure that I decided to pave but attempted to enliven with a *bocca* of a dolphin's head spouting water in the midst of the far wall. Near to the house there was a rudimentary trellis screen of three Gothick arches and a scattering of small beds accommodating climbers to smother both it and the surrounding walls. But it always remained essentially a garden of containers and this is what Julia married into, a world of pots, one of which already contained a descendant of Dooks's precious rosemary. Under her aegis the pots multiplied. Soon there was a wide range of culinary herbs, sage, rue, thyme and marjoram, as well as geraniums grown from cuttings that were set against the silvery-grey foliage of *Senecio cineraria* (syn. *Cineria maritima*), as a foil to their pink and scarlet flowerheads. Over thirty years on, much of this garden is still with us, for the containers left with the furniture on the final removal day. Brighton also marked my first encounter with box, for among those pots were two containing handsome glossy-green cones under a metre in height. These I planted here where we can still see them each day from our breakfast-room window, significant sentinels, now more than two metres high, silhouetted against a beech hedge flanking the entrance to the Small Orchard.

OVERLEAF *The view across the Knot Garden
to the front of the house*

If my horticultural credentials were minimal, Julia's were far more robust. The Oman house at Putney was one of those substantial residences built for the professional classes not long after 1900 and set into a quarter of an acre of land. At the back a broad raised terrace afforded a panorama of lawn with a lion from Barry's Houses of Parliament (whose particular history I will later retail) as its focal point, flanked by a quince tree to the left and a plum to the right. This tableau was surrounded by borders filled with a spring and summer display of flowers with a shrubbery backing. There were other fruit trees – a Cox's and 'Devonshire Quarrenden' apple and an 'Oullins Gage' – and a greenhouse and vegetable garden. My mother-in-law Joan Oman was trained as a teacher at the Froebel Institute. There much stress was laid on the value of building on a child's natural curiosity about the world around him. So it was that my wife and her brother were brought up to understand the nature of plants. Each had a little garden of their own and the vegetables they cultivated as children would be carefully harvested and cooked to be eaten. Self-sufficiency and a sense that the garden was a part of domestic economy was a given. My father-in-law tended the vegetables, keeping the kitchen supplied with spinach in particular. A 'Brown Turkey' fig, given to him by the composer Gerald Finzi, with whom he shared war work, was trained across the back of the house and, as the fruit ripened, it would be picked and displayed temptingly on a dish on the dining-room table.

Julia's love affair with the garden, therefore, began young. Not long ago, riffling through papers kept by her mother, she came across the 'magazine' she had compiled at seven and a half. Page three has the heading 'my garden' and a short essay of sorts follows: 'I do love my garden it really is fun I have got soum seedes and I have got soum sun flowrs in it to and I have got soum red roses to.'

The orthography belongs to the world of Daisy Ashford, but the sentiments are clear. On the bottom half of the page there is what I take to be a stalk with a solitary bloom at its summit and, at its side, Julia's earliest self-portrait.

Memory is a sacred attribute in any garden and our first herbaceous plants came from Putney, bright scarlet poppies and brilliant orange daylilies among them. Although the colours may jangle I would not be without them for all the world. Each year when they spring again to life and flower I think of that Putney garden, now long gone, and of the graciousness of my in-laws to the man who ran off with their daughter.

Four plants in particular speak of a special continuity, for cuttings or suckers from them now flourish in The Laskett garden. One is the 'Albertine' rose with its nearly double coppery-pink blooms. That was trained over arches across pathways, and a cutting from it now clambers up the facade of The Laskett, encircling my writing-room window. In summer some of its blooms impinge on the window glass itself, much to my delight. This is a real between-the-wars rose, 1921 to be exact. The other three plants all go back to Oxford and Frewin Hall. The white jasmine now engulfs a tiny summerhouse close to the house. The tender agapanthus winter in the conservatory and make their annual debut only when we are free of the threat of frosts. These succulent plants with their spiky leaves and blue flowers are now entering their third century, for they were certainly at Frewin in the late Victorian period. Their blue is of the intensity one associates only with hyacinths. Finally, and most important of all, there is the quince.

Let my wife tell that story in her own words, for in 2001 in *Country Life* she wrote its history:

My paternal grandfather, the historian Sir Charles Oman, lived in Frewin Hall, Oxford, a Brasenose College property, for some forty years from the turn of the century. Only two fruit trees grew and flourished in that unloved city garden: a mulberry, planted when my father, as a child, kept silkworms; and a quince, formidably occupying the end of the lawn, facing the house. The tree's origins I know not, but I surmise it could have been a century old, as the girth of leaf-spread was so considerable.

I still find it fascinating to attempt to conjure the origins of this extraordinary tree, whose progeny grows in our garden today. Before my grandfather died at the end of the Second World War, my father, who had an affection for it, dug up from under its skirts a sucker which he planted in our Putney garden sited, as at Frewin Hall, facing the house. Later, during the bleak days of food rationing in the late 1940s, autumnal guests would leave with the gift of a quince to add to their stewed apple.

I could not live in a garden where no quince tree grew. My father knew this and on the announcement of our discovery of a house with a garden in Herefordshire, he immediately earmarked two suitable quince suckers, which arrived at The Laskett with the furniture, much to the astonishment of the removal men. The trees are now 28 years old and this season were weighed down with fruit.

As our Frewin quinces, the name by which we still know them, started to grow and flourish, I became aware that they were not the same shape, nor did the trees grow in the same manner, as those I purchased as named varieties to place through the garden. With care I packaged three fruits and a sprig of leaves, together with a payment, to the fruit identification department of the Royal Horticultural Society at Wisley. A letter came back which left me no more certain as to our quince's variety. 'Possibly Lescovatz, a Serbian quince from Lescovata.' So to this day the tree remains firmly designated 'the Frewin quince', and we speculate as to its origins.

So it was that at last, at the end of the first week of May 1973, we came to rest at The Laskett.

THAT SUMMER WAS A KIND OF IDYLL, IN SPITE OF THE FACT THAT THE REMOVAL van carrying our furniture had crashed, reducing much of it to splinters. The sun seemed only to shine. Anyone moving into a new house in spring will share that feeling of elation, for a new life begins simultaneously with the reawakening of the world of nature. The house martins arrived the day we did and the front of the house was hung thickly with the pale violet panicles of an old wisteria. Soon the roses burst into bloom and the vegetable garden produced its cornucopia, first purple sprouting broccoli and then raspberries followed by strawberries in abundance. Everything that happened during those first summer months took on the quality of a dream, upon which the practicalities of owning and running a house and garden began only slowly to impinge. Apart from holidays that Arcadian idyll was a weekend one, for most of our time was spent in London in our rented Westminster flat.

'We have settled into Hereford very happily,' I wrote to my Dutch friend

Jan early in July. 'One sits in the sun and watches the landscape unfolding in every direction for miles untouched, or contemplates the great 1812 cedar on the front lawn [so we were told, but it must have been planted twenty years later], or one gardens.' And then follows the significant sentence: 'I have really become a passionate gardener.'

The site of the Yew Garden, winter 1974

Somehow within those opening weeks some kind of Pauline conversion had taken place, for I have to admit that I did say to Julia, when we bought the house, 'Don't talk to me about that garden.' With her accustomed taciturn wisdom she said nothing and wasn't in the least fazed when, within a couple of weeks, I donned wellington boots and was to be seen marching into the vegetable garden spade in hand.

That was necessary, for Millie Bryant's ancient jobbing gardener, Mr Gommery, had decided against continuing to garden. Suddenly we were faced with an ocean of lawn that demanded cutting. We found the solution to that in contract gardeners and it was they who saw us through this first summer when there were no dramatic changes to the existing garden. Julia created a small but necessary bed of culinary herbs close to the garage and also a flowerbed near to the house. I laboured to keep the existing vegetable garden in order and tended the rose beds. The truth of the matter was that our minds were firmly elsewhere, not only on the building works which had to be done to the house, but, in Julia's case, on the designs for her production of *La Bohème* at the Royal Opera House, and in mine, on the fact that I had set my sights on the directorship of the Victoria & Albert Museum which, by chance, had fallen vacant. My appointment as its new director was announced in September and I was to take up the post on 1 January 1974. Also in the autumn my mother-in-law tragically died too young of cancer. To her we owe our earliest present of gardening tools, and I recall when she presented me with a spade that she had covered the handle with a bag on which she had doodled my moustachioed face.

This was a year of change on every side, both public and private. The effect of the oil crisis was just beginning to bite, precipitating inflation and what was to become an increasingly turbulent decade. In the light of the appalling problems I had to cope with in my new post the creation of a garden seemed positively peripheral, although in fact it was to become a kind of salvation, seeing me through some of the darkest and most difficult years of my entire career.

I wish that I could write that both of us had a blinding vision in 1973 of the garden as it is now, but we didn't. That vision took time to formulate,

The site of the Fountain Court, winter 1974

his inexperience, for squirrels are almost as destructive as rabbits. A more seasoned gardener would want to shoot them.' Clearly I had much to learn. I was in fact already immersed in that extraordinary process so wisely designated by the great garden designer Russell Page as 'the Education of a Gardener'. And it is a consideration of that to which I must now turn the reader's attention.

Two

INSPIRATIONS AND INFLUENCES

THE FIRST PERSON EVER TO WALK ME AROUND A GARDEN OF THEIR OWN creation was Sir Cecil Beaton, the photographer, designer and diarist. He entered my life in the summer of 1967, shortly after I became Director of the National Portrait Gallery, when he agreed to a retrospective exhibition of his portrait photographs at the gallery, which was to be landmark. Through him I was introduced to another world, that of houses in the country with marvellous gardens. Reddish House, a delectable small late-seventeenth-century red-brick house, stood in John Aubrey's village of Broadchalke, not far from Salisbury. Cecil had purchased it in 1947 and the garden was a showpiece. John Morris Smallpiece, his gardener, said of him: 'He had a good instinct for gardens.' I would concur with that observation, battling as he did with terrain which had, in some places, only a few inches of topsoil. Whenever Cecil wished, for instance, to plant roses, the ground had to be excavated and soil brought in as a base. Twice a year the garden was open to the public and every effort was made to see that on those occasions it was immaculate, boasting what the Suttons' representative from Reading said was 'the best lawn in the West Country'.

In the last weekend of May 1968 I was asked for the first of several weekends that I spent with him before I married. The centrality of the garden to Cecil's life was something quite new to me and I recorded it:

> Cecil always opened up as he strode around the garden. There were the palest pink roses swagged on to garlands, long ropes worthy of a Gaiety Girl, climbers all over the house, a terrace which led on to a broad swathe of lawn and further gardens, the whole held in by rising land on which grew a concealing curtain of mature trees. There was an orchard, a wild garden with spring flowers, a broad walk to a seat flanked with wide herbaceous borders, a kitchen garden and a new little abstract lavender garden round an old sundial.

Returning with Cecil Beaton from a stroll around the garden at Reddish, July 1977

That dial now stands as the focal point of the garden we made in commemoration of the Queen's Silver Jubilee, a monument to the precious friendship I had with him. It will reappear later in this narrative. Not far from it still grows the unusual, if invasive, white willowherb Cecil obtained from a gardener in Regent's Park. 'Flowers,' I wrote in that diary entry, 'were the key to this house. No room was without them, nor dining table devoid of a bouquet.'

Anyone who has made a garden from scratch will share with me the impact that such an experience can have. It opened my mind to the possibility of something I had never even thought about, not that at that stage it was a possibility, but the seed was firmly sown that gardens, quite large ones, could be made. But I was also acutely aware that they called for labour, for Cecil had his splendid gardener, Smallpiece, plus one or two assistants. Cecil would have been wholly unconscious of the effect of that walk on me, although I know that thirty years on it would have given him pleasure to know that someone cherished his memory not so much for his photography or his designs but for his talent as a gardener.

It was his habit in the country to don a coat and a fedora hat, pick up a trug, complete with secateurs, and set off on a garden tour. Roses were his great passion and in that drawling dandified voice of his he would give a running commentary on their names and how they had flowered that year. Some, as I've already said, were trained on ropes, others clambered up fruit trees in the orchard, some he trained horizontally over wooden frames. The house was smothered in roses and, because he loved them as cut flowers in the house, there was a whole bed of 'Iceberg' with its green tinged with pink-white blossoms. Cecil certainly accounted for the early old-rose phase in the history of The Laskett garden, for his preference was always for these with their soft mutant colours, salmon-pink to white 'Penelope', apricot-pink 'Gloire de Dijon', carmine-pink 'Zéphirine Drouhin', blush-pink 'Fantin-Latour' or the vivid carmine-pink 'Königin von Dänemark'. Scent also meant much to him, so there was rosemary, lavender and lilac in abundance. Indeed I returned from that weekend laden with sprays of lilac. Spring flowers, narcissi naturalized in huge drifts, were another

With Cecil Beaton, after his stroke

major feature of Reddish, and he had strong views as to how these should be placed in huge bunches into glass vases so that their stalks could clearly be seen.

An inspiration, yes, but Reddish was never to be the kind of garden I wanted. To me it lacked mystery and surprise. Virtually everything was seen at a glance. Nor was it architectural, although there were ancient yews clipped into amorphous shapes and paths bordered by neat box hedges. But they were not the essence of the garden. If I had to characterize it I would say that it was a miniature landscape garden, one vast beguiling tableau of Englishness which spread its skirts outwards to one side of the house, enticing the visitor on through what was essentially an asymmetrical, painterly vision. The garden was held in by the land that formed the bowl in which it sat, onto whose natural undulations were embroidered plantings in the Jekyllesque manner with a careful consideration of colour combinations and a love of old cottage flowers, like hollyhocks and *Lilium candidum*. Later, after marriage and after Cecil's ghastly stroke, it was sad to see that garden cut back as the labour to maintain it could no longer be afforded. On one visit we saw the wide herbaceous borders being turfed over and came away with a box of herbaceous plants. Our last visit to him was in October 1979. He died two and a half months later. For me it was the end of an era. To him I owe my first horticultural stirrings.

Although I was aware of the kitchen garden at Reddish it somehow never figured much in Cecil's garden vision. He belonged to that vanished world in which people were seemingly unable even to make a cup of instant coffee. John and Myfanwy Piper offered the sharpest of contrasts for they were practical, hands-on people used to catering for themselves. I had worshipped John Piper's paintings since childhood. They offered the pastoral vision of England, bred of the Second World War, which I have always cherished, whose essence was the manor house, the parish church, the village and the embracing landscape. It was patriotic, picturesque, deeply romantic and fiercely insular. I still have in a folder one of my youthful essays in the Piperesque style, using watercolour and crayon in an attempt to depict the tomb of Sir Henry Norris in

With John Piper at Fawley Bottom, June 1976

Westminster Abbey. That was when my career was firmly pointed in the direction of the practising arts, a path which family impoverishment was to deny me. Myfanwy, his wife, was new to me but I quickly learnt that I was in the presence of a Betjeman heroine and one of Benjamin Britten's most distinguished librettists.

My earliest memory of them was of walking up to the flint and brick farmhouse at Fawley Bottom one golden evening and seeing John sitting like an Old Testament prophet on a bench with Myfanwy at his side, shelling peas from the garden into the capacious kitchen bowl on the table before him. Thirty years on I'm still mesmerized by that simple image. Few people's living style have I wished to emulate more, for its innate modesty and lack of pretension, its belief in honest work and for the focus of any artist's house to be the facilitation of creativity.

Julia had known them both from childhood, for her mother and her sisters had purchased a nearby farm for Dooks, their beloved nanny. Sometimes, when Julia was there, young Mr Piper would drive by and give her a lift into nearby Henley. Fawley Bottom they had moved into the year that I was born and I first glimpsed it not long after marriage. It was a magic place and I remember coming away thinking that that was how I wished us to live at The Laskett. But what kind of influence did their garden exert on me? This was after all far from formal; on the contrary, it was rambling and relaxed, crammed with herbs and cottage garden flowers and unashamed about the weeds springing up. Its real heart was the kitchen garden, with its rectangular beds filled with neat lines of cabbages, potatoes, onions, leeks and runner beans bordered by an explosive tapestry of species roses and flowering shrubs set against the verdant landscape beyond. One was overwhelmed by its sheer profusion. But everything was held together in the way only an artist can by the exertion through his hands of his aesthetic eye, much like Monet at Giverny. This was an artist's garden.

That evening I remember John's pride in the line of giant sunflowers he had sown and brought to their full glory. They were almost incandescent in the evening sunlight. But the prime lesson here was of the interconnection of garden and kitchen, for

With John Piper in The Kitchen Garden

the peas were not the only home-grown ingredient that was consumed at dinner that evening. Myfanwy was an inspired cook and it was John's kitchen garden that stays in my memory. It was to be one of the major inspirations behind what I regard as my wife's kitchen garden, and perhaps the effect was more potent on her aspirations for our garden, for I have always been the cook.

THOSE VISITS TO THE PIPERS OCCURRED AT PRECISELY THE PERIOD WHEN WE HAD to reach decisions about what kind of garden The Laskett would be. That was in fact determined by a group of gardens I came to know in the first few years after marriage. The first was King John's Hunting Lodge at Odiham, near Basingstoke, the creation of the great decorator John Fowler. Later, when I came to know David Hicks, the stylish interior decorator and passionate gardener, he too saluted this garden as his prime inspiration. Julia had known John from her filming days, when the Lodge had been used as a location for Tony Richardson's film *The Charge of the Light Brigade*. Julia had the task of redecorating its interior back to the 1850s. John was someone new in my life, a benign and tetchy figure, but someone who had created the style which in the eighties was to be disseminated around the globe as the English country-house style. John's decoration of his own tiny house was a distillation of the essence of his taste, fresh, restrained, with an abundant use of glazed chintz and dragged paint together with a superb deployment of drapery. There was nothing flashy about the Fowler look. Nor was there about the man, who was a mine of information on interior decoration and a monument to understatement of a kind his many imitators never quite achieved. He pioneered the whole topic of the restoration of historic interiors in such a way that in his last years he was brought in to advise the National Trust.

We stayed there in December in 1971, just three months after our wedding. The time of year is important, for my first experience of the Hunting Lodge was in winter. Once more I was moved to put pen to paper:

> But the garden is the thing. An avenue of pleached hornbeam leads to the brick facade. There are little lead statues of shepherds flanking it, pretty flower-beds with wire obelisks, and in the middle of the garden there are two Gothic gazebos of trellis which face each other. And there's John's latest addition, a large garden-room, both beautiful and comfortable, with windows looking onto a lake and a box-hedge garden.

in the ballet the same period lived again, through Julia's quite miraculous scenery and costumes, evoking the interior of the composer Sir Edward Elgar's Worcestershire house, its garden and the elm-filled landscape beyond. At the opening a gauze dissolves to reveal a quite magical tableau of late Victorian country life caught in a golden autumn early evening light. The mood is melancholy, Chekhovian. A lady lies in a hammock to one side with a young man in a straw boater leaning over her. At one moment a few stray autumn leaves flutter to the ground. Children bowl hoops and a gentleman arrives on a period bicycle. Each of Elgar's friends pictured within, as he subtitled the composition, danced their variation. I recall Dame Ninette de Valois saying at Ashton's memorial service in Westminster Abbey that this ballet and the other Julia was to do with him, *A Month in the Country* (to which I will return), were his greatest delineations of human psychology and relationships in terms of the dance. This is a poignant, moving ballet, which portrays one man's quest in his art, which ends happily with the arrival of a telegram telling of the acceptance of his score. I have never been able to see it danced without the tears welling in my eyes. Gardens are the fruits of security and I wanted The Laskett garden to conjure up its own golden age, resonating with the one we had lost.

Gardens Old and New embodied, therefore, atmosphere. It wasn't practical, for there were no ground or planting plans nor any attempt to tackle practicalities. For those I turned to another book, again one which has since been reissued, *Gardens for Small Country Houses* by Gertrude Jekyll and Lawrence Weaver. First published in 1912 and firmly a child of that era, my edition was the fourth, dated 1920. This not only dealt with the different, component, parts of a garden – steps and stairways, water, walls, paving, pergolas and so on – but also gave the ground plans and planting details of a series of what were then thought of as small gardens. Today they would be classified as large but, in fact, they were roughly the size of the domain we had available to develop. Their style inevitably is Jekyllesque, that is, with strong geometry at ground level and equally strong vertical built and evergreen architecture. Both were softened by the rich planting typical of the Jekyll style and went through her classic progression, working from formality around the house gradually outwards to wild woodland planting. These gardens too were visions, but ones I could see were of a hands-on practical variety, with enough information provided for me to crib ideas here and there, which I did.

Two other books were important to me. One was Reginald Blomfield's *The Formal Garden in England*, published in 1892. At the time I was wholly ignorant of the furore that this publication unleashed in the late Victorian gardening world, causing the venerable William Robinson, Jekyll's mentor and author of one of the great garden classics, *The English Flower Garden*, to fire off rockets in rage. In Blomfield's view the landscape style had deprived buildings of their proper settings and this now demanded reformation by the reassertion of the architect's role in the garden. At this juncture all of that passed me by. All I knew was that this was one of the two books in print on the making of formal gardens. The other, to which I'll come shortly, appeared in 1902. It is extraordinary to think that no new book on the subject was to appear until the modest one I wrote in 1989, *Creating Small Formal Gardens*. Blomfield's book argued for the land around any house to be divided up architecturally into rooms and corridors and compartments. It was a call to reinstate the old gardens of Tudor and Stuart England with their mounts and knots, arbours and palisades, galleries and pleached avenues, statues and topiary. Unlike *Gardens for Small Country Houses* this book was illustrated not by photographs but by a beguiling series of line drawings, many in fact re-drawings from old engravings, by F. Inigo Thomas. They were, however, deeply evocative. Many were reinterpretations of the bird's eye views of the great gardens of late Stuart England, as recorded in Jan Kip's *Britannia Illustrata* (1707). Soon I began to buy odd original prints as they turned up, ones which I eventually framed and which now hang in my bathroom as perpetual sources of inspiration.

For me a line-drawing aerial view beats both a photograph and a ground plan when it comes to suggesting the eventual reality of a garden composition. The pictures in Blomfield's book presented large-scale gardens which seemed to me to be perfectly manageable in terms of very limited labour. They consisted of grass, paved and gravel paths, built architectural elements, avenues of trees and plants, such as evergreens, cut into hedges or repeat shapes, like cones or drums. Using such a repertory I thought order and visual excitement could be conjured out of a large piece of land, but of a kind that would only demand mowing through the growing season and giving a once-a-year cut and prune to the trained elements. Moreover, such a garden could be planted and slowly grow, and only as and when they could be afforded need the statuary and built parts be added. Whereas most people's reaction on seeing these illustrations would have been one of

It was not to be until the eighties that I began regularly to visit these great masterpieces of formal design, but they had already left their imprint on my imagination through Georgina Masson's book. Over the last twenty years and more I have returned again and again from these unforgettable seminal creations, such as the Villa Lante at Bagnaia or the Villa Farnese at Caprarola, always fired by their extraordinary beauty, their masterly way of orchestrating a terrain, their architectural majesty of concept. Of course we could aspire to nothing of such splendour, but here were endless lessons to be learnt about the disposition of space, above all the handling of ascent and descent, for that was the great architect Bramante's invention when he first terraced the garden of the papal Villa Belvedere, now part of the Vatican in Rome, at the very opening of the sixteenth century. It was the sheer unashamed theatricality of these gardens that appealed to me, their fantasy and their concern with meaning as well as design. There was nothing tame about them. What was more, they re-emphasized the importance of firm structure, for however decayed and badly maintained an Italian garden, it was still beautiful because its geometry always remained intact.

There are three to which we still often return. The first is the Villa Lante, an extravaganza constructed for the Cardinal Gambara in the 1560s, an allegory of the loss and search for the restoration of the Golden Age as described in Ovid's *Metamorphoses*, spilling down a hillside not far from Viterbo. I have never been much interested in the classic English progression of the dissolution of garden into woodland and then into the landscape around. Bearing in mind what farmers could do, I knew that The Laskett garden had to be wholly self-contained and inward-looking, a segment carved out of the landscape. The Villa Lante is exactly that, a walled rectangle, its interior an essay in symmetry with those classic ingredients of the Italian garden, a firm central axis and a number of cross axes linked by steps and terraces and by the deployment of water splashing downwards through fountains and rills towards a spectacular parterre at the bottom. Alas, I knew that we would never be able to afford water on this scale, nor did the sharp frosts of England allow it.

The second is the Villa Farnese at Caprarola for the *palazzina*, a banqueting house away from the two main winter and summer gardens, reached by means of a rising woodland walk. I cannot imagine anything more breathtaking in garden design than the approach to this ensemble: a

OPPOSITE *Inspiration: view of the water parterre at the Villa Lante*

monumental staircase, flanked by grottoes, down the centre of which a rill falls from two recumbent river gods. At the top this leads on to a box garden around the small palazzo lined with incredible herms rearing up and piercing the blue sky and, on the other side, reached by yet another ascent, a garden of fountains. The element of surprise in garden-making is all-important here. Can anything cap what you have just seen? And here, of course, it does, for the sightlines are perfectly controlled so as never to spoil the sense of constant revelation as you climb upwards. Our earliest visits were to a garden all but abandoned. Since then it has been restored and the innumerable fountains, jets and rills of water once more sparkle in the sunshine.

Finally there is Bomarzo, the famous *Sacro Bosco* or sacred wood, created by Vicino Orsini in the 1550s. This is quite unlike anything else, a kind of mad counter-statement to the order of the renaissance garden, for here everything is asymmetrical and the visitor meanders through a wood encountering dragons and monsters, huge giants and vast recumbent figures – not to mention an elephant, an ork, a vast tortoise together with a threatening hellmouth, and a serenely classical church in an allegory which has so far defied interpretation. Many of these ghostly apparitions are sculpted from the rock that arises from the terrain. What was the lesson learnt from this astounding creation? Still it speaks across the centuries of the need for madness in the garden, for fantasy. As I get older I see its value more and more, for it embodies a release from convention, telling the gardener to defy it and let his imagination run riot. During the initial phases of The Laskett garden it was the order and calm of the renaissance garden that remained the prime inspiration. In its later phases, Bomarzo has been a spur to invent and stand the world on its head.

Other gardens, of course, contributed to the making of The Laskett, but not in its initial planning. Two in particular spring to mind. One is Het Loo, that miraculous restoration and recreation of the great late-seventeenth-century baroque garden of William III at Apeldoorn in the Netherlands. We were there in 1979 when they were excavating the terrain, peeling off the layers added to transform it into a *jardin anglais* at the beginning of the nineteenth century and revealing the fountain basins, paths and terraces of the original garden. That restoration was not to be completed until 1984,

OPPOSITE *The ascent to the* palazzina *at Caprarola as it appears in Georgina Masson's* Italian Gardens

With David and Glyn plotting the Field, 1975

structural project the split was generally fifty-fifty. But I need hardly point out that theatre design, for all its seeming high glamour, is a poorly paid profession, not that museum work is much better. Indeed, in the late seventies my salary was frozen, so that the heads of department within the museum were earning more than its director. As my second career took off, first as a consultant to Olimpia & York on the public spaces in the Canary Wharf development in the Docklands, and latterly as a professional writer, the built structure, envisioned from the outset, began, piecemeal, to be put in place. The success of first *The Story of Britain* in 1996 and then the *Diaries* the following year facilitated major changes and the addition of significant sculptural ornament. Nonetheless, it has to be said at the outset that the financial resources behind the creation of this garden have never been other than modest. Each addition and innovation has had to be carefully phased and tightly budgeted. Ingenuity with seemingly disparate materials has been one of the keys to some of the garden's most spectacular effects.

Although the second half of the seventies was marked by roaring inflation, we were fortunate in one major fact, that plants remained relatively cheap. A random invoice for trees lies before me. It is from the forester who was attached to the Lucas-Scudamore estate at Kentchurch (the Scudamores are one of the oldest families in the county) and lists twenty-five *Thuja plicata*, six *Robinia pseudoacacia*, along with eight specimen trees, including conifers, a *Ginkgo biloba*, a Swedish whitebeam and a *Koelreuteria*, all for the princely sum of £17.

Labour is as pertinent as financial resources. When we arrived we began with David and Glyn, gardeners who came one day once a fortnight from a firm of contractors, a service offered by a local garden centre. Their task above all was to mow during the growing season. Soon one of them, David, decided to set up his own little business with a colleague, Terry, who was eventually succeeded by Wilf. If we were lucky, Wilf would come on his own for a day in between their joint visits. In the winter, the mowing over, they went on to what we called projects. These could vary from digging new beds to laying paving. Anyone who has relied on a labour force of this kind will know how elusive those who give it can be. So desperate do you become to retain their services that you will put up with almost anything. Their most irritating habit was miraculously to avoid ever coming in summer on a day when we would be here. On the whole, looking back, we must be grateful to them for keeping us going during the years when the garden was in its infancy.

David was a beaming rubicund countryman, one of those people in whose hair one would expect still to find the brush, a mobile bundle of grubby working clothes with the buttons, often as not, fastened in the wrong places. He wore the same clothes the whole year round, for I was always struck how in summer he looked fit for the Antarctic. A number of his teeth were artificial but it was entirely arbitrary as to whether he would remember to put them in or not. David combined a love of Wagner with an attractive haziness, which from time to time could result in such disasters as digging in a bed of newly planted fruit bushes which Julia had just shown him with the injunction to respect them. Nor was she to forget the cherry trees, given her by her father, which he cheerfully mowed over, although, when this was pointed out, he arrived on his next visit with a gift of plants. He had a permanent expression of puzzled surprise and amazement.

Wilf, who was a builder and not a gardener, was endowed with a genuine sweetness of nature. Small of body, hesitant, shy and thoughtful, it was he who carried out our first modest ventures in hard landscaping. I can see him still with his knitted pixie hood, which I don't recollect as ever being washed, and his T-shirt with a woodpecker blazoned on it (the logo of the greatest local industry, Bulmer's Cider), which was worn beneath a jacket several sizes too big for him. But he always gave a degree of careful consideration to everything he did.

Well intentioned they certainly were, but any idea of the exact measurement of anything was wholly alien to their way of thinking. Although given specific instructions as to the proportions, for instance, of the trench for the Rose Garden hedge, the result was not the rectangle I had asked for but a rhomboid, just enough out of true for me to be preoccupied ever since with working out how to deflect the eye from the fact. In the same way they would be told to plant trees at an exact distance

The Serpentine Walk is cut, 1975

67

apart. But, oh no, that was not how they thought. Wilf, in his role as number two, would stand silently by as David would pace out the distances with his large feet encased in wellington boots. The result, of course, was that no two of the lengths were ever the same. Some would be eight, others nine and some even ten or eleven feet apart. No matter; gardening, as I've learnt through bitter experience, is the art of fudging it. David's most recurring chant still rings in my ear: 'Yes, Dr Strong,' signalling that sometimes he had taken in what I'd said and sometimes he had not.

But over the years what they charged gradually escalated until, in 1992, we reached the decision that, if we could provide the accommodation for such a person, it would be far more economical to go over to a gardener who would be more or less full-time. By that we asked for four days a week. So it was that Robin Stephens arrived. He is summed up in a note I made in my Garden Diary at the close of that year: 'Robin is a slow worker, but he has a far greater attention to detail in every way.' He was not a trained gardener, but having had a miscellaneous career from hairdresser to general factotum in another country house, he did have an eye and was dedicated to tidiness. That was reflected above all in his appearance. He was always

BELOW   *The site of the future Fountain Court and*
Small Orchard as we found it, 1973

The Yew Garden, summer 1975

immaculately turned out for the job, his thin frame in addition giving his every movement an elegance. His timekeeping was beyond reproach. We could have set our watches by his appearance in the morning as much as by his exit in the evening.

With someone four days a week we were able to make rapid advances during the five years he was with us. Then, when we had to search for a successor, we discovered that we could actually afford a properly trained gardener – and that was when Shaun Cadman arrived. The advent of someone knowledgeable and fascinated by plants was just what a maturing garden needed, for the infrastructure was fully grown and it was time to enrich the planting. Nonetheless, bearing in mind that the garden now extends to four acres and that it depends on Shaun and ourselves, it is no mean achievement.

What this constant struggle over resources taught us was to be relaxed. Gardening on the grand scale, as this inevitably became, is not that close-focus, and I soon learnt that no one is going to notice the weeds if the overall *coup de théâtre* is dramatic enough. Their eyes will simply be deflected from the shortcomings. Also, it is pointless getting agitated over when and if things get done. Early on I began resolutely to ignore those gardening columnists who were forever telling me the jobs in the garden for each week. If I had acted on their injunctions I would have abandoned the pursuit years ago. In the early stages I would carefully note what had to be done. So, give or take a bit, things were done as and when the labour came and also when we were there for any length of time beyond two or three days, which was generally for periods over Christmas, Easter and especially August. A trained horticulturalist would, I am sure, be horrified by what I cheerfully pruned in August, but it had to be, or at least it had to be until 1987, after which date we lived here. Before then both of us were at the peak of our careers in highly demanding professions. In my case gardening was the antidote to ploughing through mountains of paper. I never cease to give thanks for discovering its healing qualities. With my hands happily in the soil every trauma would be quickly soothed or slip away.

August above all was the magic month when we were here for four whole weeks, apart from a brief trip to London to clear the desk. That was the period each year during which I cut the yew hedges and the topiary and

She very much took in the originality of The Laskett. I remember her, for instance, looking at one of our beech hedges which had 'windows' cut into it. It was something Lanning Roper had told her to do to the ones at Barnsley. As she stared at them she suddenly realized what Lanning had meant, because to make a window, trunks, acting as glazing bars, had of course to be left in situ to support the hedge higher up. That caught her eye for detail, but I think what amazed her the most was the vast scale of it all and its unashamed theatricality.

Rosemary would always arrive at The Laskett with a gift of plants, and we would never leave Barnsley without some treasure in the back of the car. Often they were more than generous ones, like four-foot-high, ready-trained, golden box cones, which would have cost a small fortune from any nursery. She instinctively knew that whatever it was it was going to an appreciative home. My Garden Diary occasionally records the advent of such gifts. In 1987 in April I noted: Planted Rosemary Verey's plants... *Thymus vulgaris* 'Silver Posie', *Salvia argentea* and *Lychnis coronaria* 'Alba'. Two months later again: Planted Rosemary Verey's plants: *Salvia sclarea* var. *turkestanica*, *Aster novae-angliae* 'Andenken an Elma Pötschke' and *Lychnis flos-jovis*. She was always 'discovering' plants. One year it would be bidens, another a ground-cover salvia with the prettiest blue flowers, and yet another attempting to restore golden privet to favour. All of these enthusiasms left their mark permanently or temporarily on our garden. But the most refreshing quality she had, as far as I was concerned, was that she was someone with whom I could walk around the garden and have a serious constructive conversation.

In 1998 she was eighty and the occasion was marked by a series of fêtes; we went to all three. One was a dinner at the Tate Gallery on Millbank, the second another dinner, this time at the Garrick Club, and the third, a surprise, to which the Prince of Wales came, was on a private aerodrome in Gloucestershire. At the time I wrote:

This is 'Rosemary Verey is eighty' week. Although that doesn't actually happen until 21st December no less than three parties are being held in her honour. Two were London-based, one at the Tate Gallery given by its chairman, David Verey, a remote connexion, and the other by Arthur Reynolds [an

OPPOSITE *Windows cut into a beech hedge with glimpses through to the Yew Garden*

American friend of Rosemary's] at the Garrick Club, courtesy of me. The first was for *tous les grands*, or as *tous* as could be garnered, mainly those whose gardens had figured in Rosemary's television series, like the Carringtons, the Cavendishes, the Astors and the Tollemaches... The next night some twenty gathered at the Garrick, a much cosier occasion and really far more enjoyable... Still one must be grateful for Rosemary. One owes her so much and she soldiers on, a brave spirit.

Brave spirit indeed. I somehow knew, two years later, that when she went into Cheltenham Hospital with a perforated intestine that would be the end, and so it proved to be. During that anxious period I made a point of sending her a pretty postcard as often as I could, for the sick gain much from being remembered by those still caught up in the rush of daily life. Usually in no state to read, they gain joy from looking at the picture. In her case it was always one of a garden or a flower.

I was honoured and touched to be asked by the family to give the keynote address at her service of thanksgiving held in a packed church in Cirencester on 24 July 2001. This is what I said:

I only knew Rosemary from her sixties onwards. My lasting vision of her is of a lady in a silk dress, her neck swathed in pearls, her hair immaculate, a gracious if at times a formidable presence. To foreigners she fulfilled exactly their dream image of an English country gentlewoman, one who would then promptly don sensible shoes and a quilted jacket and traipse around the garden. I think that she was fully conscious of meeting such expectations for visitors to Barnsley. Although she always mourned the loss of David, widowhood in a way gave Rosemary a new lease of life, enabling her to respond fully to her role as a star of the horticultural world. And she loved every minute of it.

What were the roots of Rosemary's distinctive garden style? Her native Gloucestershire must rank high, for she lived and gardened in that part of England which had seen the creation of some of the great gardens of the Arts and Crafts Movement in the decades before 1914. Those impulses are summed up in Rodmarton Manor, in which all the threads that formulated that style are still entwined: memories of William Morris with his advocacy of native plants, the plea for formality of Reginald Blomfield, whose *The Formal Garden in England* held up the manor-house gardens of the Tudor

OPPOSITE *Elizabeth Tudor in late autumn*

George was a Pakenham, an intellectual dynasty of which at least one other member had a horticultural passion. Dendrological would perhaps be the better word, for George's cousin Thomas, the present Lord Longford, who gave the funeral address, was not only a distinguished historian but also the author of the bestseller *Meetings with Remarkable Trees*. Thomas and George used to trump each other's aces over the trees they had seen and occasionally in the book George can be spied as the anonymous figure in the photograph, placed by his cousin to establish the scale of a particular tree. Green fingers were also inherited by George's sister, Alice, Viscountess Boyd, a member of the Council of the Royal Horticultural Society and the chatelaine of a five-acre garden at Ince Castle at Saltash in Cornwall. Through her marriage into the Lennox-Boyds we came to meet her sister-in-law, Arabella Lennox-Boyd, a garden designer of great distinction, the winner of a succession of gold medals at the Chelsea Flower Show and the creator of a remarkable garden of her own at Gresgarth in Lancashire.

But what of Whitfield? Whitfield was purchased by the Clive family in 1796. It had already been landscaped by that date with oak groves and a beech walk. Edward Bolton Clive was a friend of Uvedale Price, one of the major proponents of the new Picturesque garden style at the close of the eighteenth century. Tree planting must have run in the Clive family for the giant Redwoods at Whitfield had been planted by the Rev. Archer Clive in the year of the Great Exhibition, 1851, twenty of them, the biggest in any group in Britain. The seeds had only arrived in Britain in 1843, eight years before, and the tallest is now 148 feet high. In 1872 it was written that 'the great charms of Whitfield are to be found in the sylvan scenery amid which it is situated, and the pleasant air of tranquillity which pervades it'. That was still true of it under George's aegis at the close of the twentieth century. Educated at Eton and Christ Church, Oxford, the shy but stubborn

George had come into this vast estate as a child. The depradations of death and tax had left it in a sorry state, from which his mother rescued it post-war, tearing down the two vast Victorian wings and returning it to its elegant Georgian proportions. George was to leave his mark not on the house but across the acres that surrounded it.

Whitfield glimpsed across the lake

George Clive and a magnolia, spring 1998

With George I found myself in contact with a very different tradition from the suburban gardening of my childhood or the garden-making of the kind I'd experienced at Reddish or King John's Hunting Lodge or at Oving. This was a man who thought in terms of landscape gardening, of planting woods, groves, copses, avenues as well as specimen trees over hundreds of acres. It was gardening of a vastly different kind from The Laskett, but that was irrelevant. There was huge exhilaration to be had from knowing someone who could still garden in the eighteenth-century terms we associate with 'Capability' Brown and Repton.

The area at Whitfield which we knew best, however, was that around the house. At the back French windows opened out from the library dining-room onto a stone terrace flanked by pleached limes. This led onto a large rectangle of immaculately kept lawn held in by an old yew hedge, topped by whimsical topiary. Beyond lay parkland. This was the site of what once must have been an Edwardian flower garden, long since grassed over, but to which George added a handsome fountain, which came from Copt Hall, Essex, as a focal point. Strange to say I do not recall ever having seen that fountain working. I always longed for him to put back a formal garden here once again, but, true to the thrust of his horticultural interests, he never did. It was not that he was uninterested in other forms of garden-making, quite the contrary, but his vision was firmly elsewhere.

I once recorded him thus: 'He was a large, fair-haired, blue-eyed man with a stammer which only left him when he spoke on the telephone. He was a born countryman, all tweeds and corduroy worn out of shape and totally unconscious of his appearance... He loved his garden and had a phenomenal knowledge of trees and plants.' To that one can add agriculture, contemporary literature and history, for he was hugely well read. In that sense he was the quintessence of the old country-house owner who was expected not only to know how to manage his estates productively but also to be a person of intellectual cultivation. The last fact explains why dinner at Whitfield was always an occasion to be savoured, for there was sure to be good and informed conversation, with an interesting assembly of guests. His talents were recognized, for he was on the National Trust's Estates and Gardens panels and was a great force behind the National Council for the

Conservation of Plants and Gardens, acting for a period as its secretary for our part of the country. The estate itself was a pioneering model in terms of good husbandry and plant conservation, wild flowers being close to George's heart.

His creation we knew best was the approach to the house, for the drive was lined with a handsome avenue of mature lime trees, which he had planted as a young man and which had grown so well that he was able to take out alternate trees. Driving along that avenue, one caught glimpses to the left of his reordering of the terrain in the front of the house, which was sited on the summit of a gentle slope. There was already a pond in front of it, but in 1968, when he was still only in his late twenties, George enlarged that. Seven years later a canal was excavated to lead to a new, even larger pond, which was dotted with islands, on one of which there was a ruined castle and whose focal point was a large statue of a warrior silhouetted against the horizon. Much of this George had created with his own hands, lugging around huge boulders and siting them to effect. Standing in front of the house this was an extraordinarily bold, painterly composition: the waters, framed by trees, stretching into the distance shimmering in the light, and the eye taken even further by an avenue of poplars disappearing towards the horizon. In the middle of the first pond he had introduced a *jet d'eau*, thrusting up, I would guess, ten metres or so. As far as I could deduce, it was only put on for visitors. Sometimes he would forget to do it, and then say, 'Just a minute,' disappear, and then, suddenly, up it would shoot into the air. His last project had been a bubbling fountain in the forecourt of the house, which was to act as a source for the whole composition.

This was garden-making of a far different kind from any other we had so far encountered, reminding us that gardening is a many-roomed mansion. When The Laskett was opened for the first time for a few days to small groups, I suggested it was twinned with a visit to Whitfield, as the contrast was so very striking. It set our garden, by then billed as the largest formal garden to be planted since 1945, sharply into context. Compared with the rolling acres of Whitfield it was minute.

The interchange with Whitfield was constant, so much so that we took it for granted. Only once did I put pen to paper to capture something of it as a garden experience. The entry is for 15 March 1998:

Spring came remarkably early this year, February in fact, which, after weeks of deluge, was marked by warmth and sun on such a scale that by early March we found the peach trees already in blossom. So it was no surprise when we found a message on the answerphone from George Clive asking us to lunch at Whitfield. 'The magnolias are at their prime.' George Clive is a tree man and has a park to boot, for it is really no use being the one without the other. He's seen our garden since it was a blank field. When we came in 1973 I recall his mother, Lady Mary Clive, ringing and asking us for tea. She was there today, aged ninety, her brain as sharp as ever...

It's difficult to think that the house was abandoned in the thirties because of the disappearance of staff or that the Victorian wings were demolished. The effect is that it's always been like that, a spacious eighteenth-century house with symmetrical bow windows set high on a slope reflected in the lake in front of it. The lake was made by George and really the garden's the thing. There are some seventy varieties of magnolia, pink, white, magenta and every variable flush of one into the other. They were superbly planted, some thrusting up to be reflected in the water, others against huge tapestries of dark green yew. On arrival we all, bit by bit, fell out of our cars and wandered around, gaping and gasping with delight as the sun caught the water and the trees. Penny Graham [George's partner]...had to leave after lunch to go to a friend who was dying of cancer. I said, 'Live every day as your last.' She said, in reply, 'Live every day as your first.' And I felt the warmth of the sun on my face and I thought that this wouldn't have been a bad last day – friends, happiness, strolling through the explosion that is spring wrapt into its beauty. The magic of the country house, its park and garden never ceases to lose its hold on me as a perfection of life.

That vignette of one visit to Whitfield encapsulates an experience relived many times over the years that we knew George. He never wrote down the names of all those varieties of magnolia. With foresight, after his death, his sister Alice sought out the magnolia expert, himself ill, and got on record what was a precious heritage. The fact of the matter was George never needed to label the trees because he knew each and every one on sight. Seventy was a huge number, for there are only eighty species of magnolia in all. Those placed around the lake were of the deciduous variety which flower in spring. George's enthusiasm for them was shared by his cousin Thomas. Somehow what would seem an appalling wait for their first flowering – thirty years in some cases – was an attraction rather than a deterrent to them both. Of course, George had the commoner shrub-like magnolias, like stellata and its hybrids, which are met with time and again as the one

His was an affectionate and knowledgeable presence, a benign influence on our garden. Above all, during those years when we were struggling to establish it, never at any point did he view what we were doing with derision, as so many of our visitors, by implication, did. Knowing the nature of plants, he knew that our fledgling garden would grow and thrive, and his letters of thanks, after many an evening spent here with dinner prefaced by the inevitable garden tour, always explode with amazement at what we had managed to achieve since his last visit. It was wholly in character for him to have imagined a tour guide to Whitfield, spying George from afar heaving some vast sandstone rock in order to build a romantic ruin on one of his islands, saying, 'And there you can see Lord Littlebrain building his own folly.' Littlebrain he was not. And, if gardening be a folly, I can think of many far worse. For us his friendship remains a haunting and potent memory. Along with Rosemary and so many other friends he lives still in The Laskett garden.

HOW CAN I END THIS INTERRUPTION TO MY NARRATIVE? WHAT WAS IT THAT these two people had in common which meant so much to us that I place them at the centre of this history? Both of them in their own way, like us, had made gardens from scratch, or almost from scratch. They understood what that involved. If I had to cite what hurt us most during all those years in which the garden grew, it was those who scoffed at us, usually behind our backs. Time and again we knew that was going on, even as we toured the garden with them staring at our sprigs of yew. The scoffers were of two kinds. The first those who knew nothing about gardens, and who had never made one. The second those with abundant financial resources, smiling condescendingly at our efforts to create this or that effect, with little at our disposal except our own ingenuity. George and Rosemary were never anything other than encouraging and understanding, knowing full well our resources in terms of money, labour and time and never despising them. Always but always they wanted to view the garden in every season, regardless of the weather, to see how things had grown, to inspect our latest project and to make helpful suggestions. And always but always too, after they had gone, we were left in a happy, grateful haze that we had been blessed with such friends.

Five

HOW DOES YOUR GARDEN GROW?

I LEFT THE READER IN 1977 WITH THE CREATION OF A GARDEN TO MARK THE Queen's Silver Jubilee and, in the last chapter, I quoted from the first article ever published about The Laskett garden by Rosemary Verey in 1987. But what happened during the intervening decade? I am often asked, 'How long does it take to make a garden?' To that I can reply, thirty years on, with some degree of authority. The answer is fifteen years. By then, with careful nurturing, even the yew hedges begin to look as though they had been planted by Gertrude Jekyll. I go on to say that the first five years are agony, with everything barely a metre high and vast gaps between trees and shrubs. Inevitably no one understands the vision in your mind's eye. You, of course, see a mighty clipped wall of velvety green hedging, whereas all the visitor to your garden sees is a row of small straggly bushes at knee height. That, I can tell you, is a testing period. The pace quickens during years five to eight. The spaces between begin, at last, to diminish, trees start roaring heavenwards and hedging shrubs at last meet. From year nine onwards no one can deny that you are creating something that must just evoke an appreciative murmur from even the most horticulturally philistine.

In this account I pass over the never-ending battles against the enemies of horticulture – rabbits, moles, squirrels, mice, pigeons, to name but a few. Add to them the constant struggle against the elements, in this case flooding, wind and killer frosts. The moles, for instance, had decided to turn the Rose Garden into Clapham Junction and we could hardly cross it without a foot collapsing into one of their tunnels. Once we skimmed the surface turf off and stood astonished at the myriad passageways running in every direction. I pass over the rage felt at seeing large mounds of soil left on what was supposed to be well-kept grass. At last I found a molecatcher, an unlikely person, Josephine, a middle-aged lady from Rose Cottage at Mansell Gamage, who arrived dressed, I always thought, like a cavalier when she came to

The avenue Elizabeth Tudor from Hartwell Grove, 1977

and again the opening lines of John Donne's *Twicknam Garden* summed up for me my relationship with the garden:

> Blasted with sighs, and surrounded with teares,
> Hither I come to seeke the spring,
> And at mine eyes, and at mine eares,
> Receive such balmes, as else cure every thing...

His was the cry of a lover in distress, mine the one of someone who felt utterly alone, but for Julia, amidst a sea of troubles.

The garden too took on another dimension during these years. It is always, I believe, greater to create than to write about creation. By that I mean, in the most rudimentary sense, that it is better, for example, to be Rembrandt than an art historian writing a book on him. Suddenly, through the garden, my urge to create in aesthetic terms, denied through circumstance in childhood, found expression. The Laskett garden was never to me anything other than a work of art in the making, one that called for vision, the exercise of the eye, the application of taste, discipline, patience, craft and knowledge over a sustained period of time to conjure up an unforgettable experience through the time-honoured application of art to nature. It was always viewed with that higher vision in mind, one of a kind I learnt about through studying garden history. There I read that any great garden was not only an arrangement of plants and artifacts in terms of design and composition but also a tissue of allusions and ideas. In our case to wander in The Laskett garden was a journey of associations. On a superficial level the garden set out to delight and surprise but, on a deeper one, for us the resonances have always been far more complex.

APART FROM THE SILVER JUBILEE GARDEN, 1977 SAW A NUMBER OF OTHER significant changes. In the middle of February I wrote in a staccato way:

> This week the hedge between Paine [the neighbouring farmer] and ourselves was reduced, cleared and tidied, gaining us at least twenty feet more of land. We look exposed! The poplar trees have been moved here as a screen. During December we replanted Elizabeth Tudor with *Nothofagus nervosa*, the first half of Mary Queen of Scots [now the Beaton Bridge leading up to the Hilliard Garden] with *Chamaecyparis lawsoniana* 'Columnaris Glauca' and turned the second half into a maze of specie roses, nearly all 'Lord Penzance'

briars from Hilliers. We planted the walk parallel to the drive to the house with *Robinia pseudoacacia*. The amelanchiers were planted in the Rose Garden and look marvellous. I enlarged the central bed and planted it thick with huge grey plants: *Brachyglottis* (Dunedin Group) 'Sunshine', *Senecio cineraria* 'White Diamond', lavender, pinks, etc. ... The roses have been trimmed into pillar roses...we planted in front of the house thuja and laurel to hem ourselves in after a cow had careered through the garden and eaten the top off the arbutus.

Poor arbutus. It never survived. And that was sad, because it was one among a trolley-load of plants I had been given as a farewell present by the staff of the National Portrait Gallery early in 1974. A party was held in my honour in my beloved Tudor gallery presided over by the famous 'Ditchley' Portrait of Elizabeth I, a silvery vision in a farthingale standing on the British Isles. On the trolley were other plants, all of them bedizened

BELOW   *The Scandinavian Grove in spring*
OVERLEAF   *The Orchard in spring*

From that the reader will have gathered how profoundly changed in character that whole area became from being a mere circle of yew in the field grass interrupting a parade of poplars. What I have not dwelt upon is the fact that this north–south axis was cursed from the outset by one almighty eyesore. In the Kitchen Garden was sited an electric junction box from which wires descended south to Laskett Cottage (The Folly). For this facility the Midlands Electricity Board paid us an annual pittance. The junction box we successfully obscured with the fast-growing x *Cupressocyparis leylandii*. The main axis presented appalling problems as I had somehow to site trees and shrubs to deflect the eye from the electric poles and overhead cables. Once, early on, I asked a representative of the electricity board to contemplate the full horror in the hope that he might take pity on us and re-site the poles in the adjacent farmer's field or bury the cables. Alas, the man who came was overbearing and officious and, far from holding out a ray of hope, instead berated me as to their right to mutilate and prune any tree or shrub of ours which dared impede access to their poles or junction box. In addition, he demanded a pathway wide enough for their lorry to career through the garden. I was both mortified and defeated.

At the time it never occurred to me to question the board's right to cross our land. It was not until over a decade later that I was to learn that the authorities, far from having the rights they claimed, were actually bound by law to provide electricity even if way leave was withdrawn. And that, in the end, was what we did. This time another of their officials appeared, someone quite unlike his predecessor, indeed who was positively benign, who was entranced by the garden and arranged for the poles to be removed and the cables buried at their expense. Ever since we have been on the best of terms with the Midlands Electricity Board. We owe this triumph to George Williams, a doughty Welshman who was creating a marvellous landscape garden in a Welsh valley near Crickhowell. The garden included a natural winding stream, a magnificent laburnum tunnel and a Chinese Chippendale bridge leading to a delightful pavilion designed by Quinlan Terry. George had already achieved the removal of similar eyesores by the simple expedient of getting a solicitor to write a letter to the electricity board withdrawing way leave. It was a tip which in my turn I was able to pass on to another garden-besotted friend, the novelist Susan Hill. In her

OPPOSITE *Arch embraced by the rose 'Phyllis Bide' in the Christmas Orchard*

frame whatever it was, and also a backcloth of conifers, common laurel and *Viburnum tinus* (laurustinus). Inevitably, in desperation, the nomadic sundial found its way there for a time, but, in 1980, something happened which resolved the yawning gap. I was awarded the Shakespeare Prize.

That prize is given annually by the FVS Foundation of Hamburg to the person considered to have contributed most to the arts in Britain. It was an incredible honour to receive such an award. The list of recipients, Henry Moore, Margot Fonteyn, David Hockney and Harold Pinter among them, reads like a roll call of those who have contributed to this country's culture during the second half of the twentieth century. I still remain the only museum person ever to be given it. The prize involved a ceremony in the town hall in Hamburg, speeches, the presentation of a medal and a handsome cheque. At the lunch given afterwards, I spoke a second time and said how I intended to commemorate this auspicious moment in my career – the first public recognition I had ever had – in the garden. And so it was that in the autumn of 1980 the Shakespeare Monument arose.

It was a reproduction in reconstituted stone of an urn designed by William Kent for Longleat House in Wiltshire. I placed it on a stone platform two steps in height. From Elizabeth R it was seen straight on, while from Mary Queen of Scots it was seen at a diagonal. In all, the urn is about three metres in height, and testimony to my fervent belief that garden ornaments should be on a large scale if they are to make any impact. From the moment we got it up I was thrilled with it. Suddenly our grand avenue had a point, for it actually led somewhere. The following spring there was real satisfaction to be gained from the vista along the sixty-yard walk of Elizabeth R. This was the most theatrical spectacle so far in the garden, the long grass either side of the walk filled with yellow daffodils with the beech trees emphasizing the perspective.

Much later, in the early nineties, we were to embellish the Shakespeare Monument. Reg Boulton, the sensitive artist craftsman who had carved the circular slate plaque for the Oman pinnacle, carved two more oval ones, which he inset into the pedestal of the Monument. On one there figured the logo of the FVS Foundation, a fountain, together with the date, 1980, while on the other he did a bas-relief of Shakespeare with the initials WS and RS below, perhaps getting a little carried away with it all. Later still we were to gild the finial and add blue and honey-yellow colour washes to delineate

OPPOSITE *The Shakespeare Monument*

Vitis coignetiae, which turns bright red, and another rose, 'Veilchenblau' ('Violet-Blue'), the nearest thing there is to a blue rose, although in truth its blooms run from purplish to bluish-violet.

This building remains the climax of any tour of The Laskett garden, a tour which takes on almost a spiritual dimension with the inscription we added later in Greek across the pediment, which in translation reads: 'Memory, mother of the Muses.' The Muses lived in a museum and memory, Mnemosyne, is the key to the garden, memory of family and friends and events which have shaped and touched both our lives. Appropriately there are heavy swags of rosemary for remembrance on either side. Mnemosyne too is the only word inscribed above the entrance to the institution to which intellectually I owe most, the Warburg Institute in the University of London. Its scope is the history of the classical tradition in the West and it was there that I spent three extraordinary years having the eyes of my mind opened under the aegis of the late Dame Frances Yates, one of whose most brilliant pioneering books was an attempt to trace the classical art of memory from antiquity to the age of the philosopher Leibniz. I owe her an incalculable debt, even though our relationship, that of professor and pupil, was not always an easy one. So the reader can understand just how complex the thoughts that assail my mind every time we sit here.

On a summer's evening we sometimes take a basket with a bottle and two glasses and make our way to the Temple. There we sit, our eyes turned towards the great sweep of the axis down to the Shakespeare Monument, whose gilt finial glints in the distance. Wine may fill the glasses but memory our minds, above all in my case, the recollection of all those years as director of the museum I fell in love with as a child and which it was my privilege to direct for fourteen years during the second half of the twentieth century. There we sit, not saying very much to each other but in perfect accord, watching, as Lindy Dufferin told me to, our garden grow.

In June, not long after the Temple was finally up, Anne Scott-James came over with Rosemary Verey to visit the garden, see what she had never seen when she had written her article and discover whether I had come to terms with squirrels as vermin. She wrote a letter to her daughter Clare describing the experience in her delightful book, *Gardening Letters to my Daughter* (1990).

OPPOSITE *The Victoria & Albert Museum Temple amid a froth of roses*

BELOW *Little Sparta: a garden of the mind*

1.30 p.m. for the interview, but we wandered in the garden first. I was quite unprepared for its scale, which is modest, a mosaic of small contained areas and meandering paths with trees, shrubs and much low-maintenance planting. The garden comes as such a surprise, for the approach is up an ascent through three farmyard gates and along a rough track. There it sits at the end, on the hillside, like some symbolic aberration. Ian Hamilton Finlay suffers from agoraphobia and never leaves his domain, learning about the world around him through books and photographs. Perhaps this accounts for the scale of the myriad sculptures and inscriptions peppered across the landscape. Everywhere one walks there are tiny columns or plaques or strange gate piers, like the ones bearing hand grenades. There is such a plenitude as one wanders up and down through what is an extraordinary fantasy world surrounding a small lake. It is like a contemporary Bomarzo: a huge gilded head of Apollo stares up from the ground, trees are planted into the sculpted bases of columns, dedications here and there commemorate the painters Albrecht Dürer and Caspar David Friedrich and the heroes and villains of the French

Revolution. There are many buildings and monuments, but all quite small, among them a pyramid and a grotto celebrating Dido and Aeneas. The imagination roams around the classical world with inscriptions from Ovid and others and swoops down the centuries to embrace the French Revolutionary period and then on to the condition of our own time as Hamilton Finlay sees it with strange tableaux like that on the topos *Et in Arcadia Ego* [And Death even in Arcady], which depicts shepherds discovering a tank with a skull and crossbones on it. Great use is made of columns of all kinds, both complete and broken and also capitals. A crofter's cottage looking across a pond has incised into its facade classical columns and an inscription identifying it as the Temple of the Muses.

As we skirted the pond a small elderly man appeared waving a sheet of paper. It was Ian Hamilton Finlay, a kindly, avuncular figure who spoke with a soft, almost lilting, Scottish accent. The paper was a plan of the garden and off we set again and then, on the dot of 1.30 p.m., we went to the house, a mere cottage, and carried our chairs onto the terrace to do the interview about the garden he had designed at Luton [and which I had opened], but the principles of it were also those of Little Sparta. Here is a man who left school at fourteen and who has surrounded himself with an imaginary landscape peopled with allusions which could only ever come from a deep knowledge of classical literature, the German Romantics and French Revolutionaries. He was tremendously fluent, lamenting the impoverishment of the garden in our own age, one whose basis was the colour supplement and television. In the past the garden was a point of departure and a setting for profound ideas, esoteric ones, and he cursed those who had let education slide so that even allusions so elementary as those to Apollo and Daphne could no longer be understood. But his was an extraordinarily benevolent view of things, for all he wanted of his visitors was for them to enjoy the garden. I asked him whether it mattered to him that they did not understand it. No, he replied, there are many levels of understanding and none was to be despised. I found it difficult to reconcile this gentle man with the image so often projected of him outside as a crypto-Nazi sympathizer who depicted Apollo holding a machine gun and not a lyre.

The garden made an enormous impression on me. There are lessons to be drawn for The Laskett. I admired the modesty of it. There was little money here and yet he has created something more significant in its way than either Sissinghurst or Hidcote, a recovery of the great tradition stretching back through William Kent to Alberti.

CONDITOR·HORTI·FELIC

I recall opening an exhibition in Hereford and two *grandes dames* approaching me and saying, 'You must be horrified at the colour those people have painted the cottage at the bottom of your drive.' To which I had to reply, 'Oddly enough, it was us.'

The English seem notoriously nervous of colour, something which does not afflict either the Welsh or the Irish. The English are also nervous of gold. Nothing as far as I'm concerned enlivens a winter's day more in a garden than a flash of gold glinting as the sun catches it. Unfortunately gold does not come cheap, so that the splashes here are relatively restrained, but I confess to my love for the gilded fountains of Versailles and Peterhof. However, with the aid of a gold-leaf-fixated student from Herefordshire College of Art we gilded the balls on Muff's Monument and on the column to Elizabeth, both to sensational effect. Since then the antlers of the recumbent Stag at the close of the great Orchard vista have been gilded. Every form of gold paint has been tried on them, but with no real success. Nothing, but nothing, can replace real 22-carat gold leaf.

SO MUCH FOR THE BUILDING, STRUCTURE AND ORNAMENTATION, BUT WHAT other major changes came in the garden during these years? One was the gradual transformation of what had been a dull turn-around for cars at the top of the drive into what we now call the Fountain Court. Up until 1988 all that had been done was to plant some handsome conifers on either side of the decaying Judas tree, which Julia would never permit me to fell. It was, I admit, seen directly from the breakfast-room window and in spring its bluish-pink flowers were a pretty sight, but all I could see, as the years progressed, were the tree's branches lurching more and more apart. And then, all of a sudden, it happened. Julia said that I could take the tree down, but on one condition, that I gave her a fountain.

On 28 August 1988 I wrote: 'Discussed fountain on mound.' This telegraphic abbreviation of intent was to be the preface to a five-year saga, one of the kind which drove me in the end to swear that I would never again employ this or that 'little man' to do something. The fountain basin was dug out in January 1989, but it was not until the same month

With David discussing the Fountain, winter 1989

two years later that I was to write 'work on the fountain'. Eventually, on 31 August 1992, comes the note: 'Mike Powell got the fountain going.' That we got it going at all was thanks to George Clive, who put us on to Mike Powell, for the odd labour we had used to erect the fountain had no clue as to how to make it function. The same year we banished the turn-around, paving and planting it, thus forming an entrance to the garden proper which fully warranted Reg Boulton's plaque inscribed 'Circumspice'.

This was the happy end of a more than tortuous saga involving small builders who came and went, one that reached its climax in the frustration which marked the initial phases of the Howdah Court and was only resolved by the arrival of Steve Tomlin. I cannot recount our elation at seeing that fountain throw up its first jet of water. Water is such a gift to any garden, and when it moves, plashes, shimmers and sparkles it is pure poetry. For us the fountain is ideally sited, for we look at it both at break-fast and lunch. In winter it is, of course, bagged against damage by frost, along with much of the other statuary. But, when we deem spring to have finally arrived, it is unveiled, serviced and then the switch controlling the pump is put on in the kitchen. Whoosh, up it goes. If any single event in The Laskett garden year signals that spring has come, this is it.

I have mentioned our visit to Gresgarth in 1993 and my lament about our lack of flowers. That lack had become something of a fixation already four years earlier. It was prompted as much as anything by a burgeoning career as a writer of books on garden design. In the case of these I had a rule never to write about anything that I had not done myself. I may not, of course, have done whatever it was successfully, but at least I had tried. Every garden book I read, for instance, seemed to contain a diagram as to how to fan-train a peach tree. Any attempt by me to apply the directions of such a diagram to one of our own trees was generally the harbinger of plant death.

But to return to flowers. In October 1989 there appears the entry: 'Began to dig Flower Garden'. That was in response not only to a keen awareness of my own ignorance, but also to the fact that now we actually lived more or less permanently in the country we could embark on such a feature, with the knowledge that we would be there not only to tend it but to enjoy the

OPPOSITE *Detail: Virginia Creeper on the wall of The Folly*
OVERLEAF *View to the Howdah Court across the Gothic ironwork screen*

garden this holds a great mystery. The Laskett garden is so many things, inseparably intertwined. It is nature tamed by art, a *jardin d'amour*, a memory system, a manipulation of space, an illusion, but over and above everything else, it is a private sacred space in which the true circle of a marriage has been tenderly inscribed. It has always been an emotional struggle as to whether to open or not, even to the smallest number. It is not that one doesn't wish to share its joys as well as its sorrows, it is the fact that the garden is so intensely personal, so enmeshed into the fabric of our very being, our actions and our thoughts, that, for the perceptive, to be allowed even a glimpse of it is to peer into the mirror of one's soul. For its creators The Laskett garden is charged with an atmosphere which is almost, at times, overwhelming in the depth and complexity of its meaning. But I wouldn't have it any other way.

What is life after all but a flower that throws up its leaves from the dark earth into the light, unfurls ever larger until, at its zenith, its petals open in response to the warmth of the sun? But such a blossom also fades and falls, to return once more to the earth from whence it sprang. And so do we. Can anything in life be more beautiful than making such a mirror of the human condition? Let Andrew Marvell speak once more for me:

> Fair quiet, have I found thee here,
> And Innocence thy Sister dear!
> Mistaken long, I sought you then
> In busie Companies of Men.
> Your sacred Plants, if here below,
> Only among the Plants will grow.
> Society is all but rude,
> To this delicious Solitude.

The garden to me is a mirror of the three greatest virtues, faith, hope and love, for to cultivate one calls for the exercise of all three. But, we are told, the greatest of them all is love and indeed how well I know the truth of that. So when the end comes all I ask for is that someone, be it Julia or a dear friend, will step out into that garden once more and break off a fair branch of rosemary to lay on my coffin, and that my ashes be scattered on the patch of God's earth which in this transitory life I have loved most.

OPPOSITE PAGE *Thirty years on*

GARDEN TOUR

OPPOSITE PAGE *Orchard walk in Springtime*

THERE IS A SET ROUTE AROUND THE LASKETT GARDEN. IN THAT sense it is within the tradition of the great landscape creations of the eighteenth century, like Stowe in Buckinghamshire, which was meant to be toured in a particular way so that the visitor should see a succession of garden pictures, each of which had meaning. The Laskett garden is by no means as precise as that, in that there is not a thought sequence but, rather, a pictorial one which moves from large to small, from wide to narrow, from light to dark, from formal to informal, from loose to tight. More important even than that, to journey around it in a particular way preserves the element of surprise so crucial to any really exciting garden experience, for the planning of the four-acre site is such that the visitor is given the illusion that the space is much larger than it really is. What follows is such a tour, moving area by area through the garden and giving details of the history of each space and of its planting. Although this is essentially 'our' garden, there are areas which are more specifically under supervision of one rather than the other of us. The more formal elements are my domain, areas like the Yew Garden, the Jubilee and Rose Gardens, Elizabeth Tudor, the Folly Garden and Covent Garden. Others I think of as more specifically Julia's: the Howdah Court, the Scandinavian Grove, Hearne's Oak Garden, the Christmas Orchard and the Kitchen Garden. Contributions are endlessly made to each other's sections, and there are parts which just seem neutral.

Although a great deal of the planting detail is included, this is not a definitive description of every single plant in the garden, bearing in mind that much thrives and withers, comes and goes and also moves, added to which, as every gardener knows, all too often the label has vanished or you've forgotten what you'd planted. By the time this appears in print plants will have been added or have migrated or, sadly, died. My wife is the plant collector. In her case through the garden are scattered almost a hundred *Malus* varieties as well as collections of historic apples (about sixty), quinces (about a dozen), snowdrops (about sixty), *Pulmonaria* (about fifty) and *Chaenomeles* (about twenty). I should add, too, that this Garden Tour does not enlarge on every memory and person who comes to mind through associations with every part and plant.

The reader is asked to follow the tour by referring to the numbered plan on the following pages.

Any tour begins with the **YEW GARDEN** [1] which stretches to the east and, when we came, was an expanse of lawn with, to one side, a shrubbery, in which a small summerhouse nestled, and, to the other, a gravel path bordered with rose beds. In the centre of the lawn, near the house, was a wellhead, a remnant of an earlier garden scheme, and the lawn stretched towards a large rectangular pond at the far end. This area was to be the site of our first garden room, the beds for the hedging being dug in August 1974 and the yew planted in December. This was to be a room with openings, the two from the house affording vistas to finials which are today atop pedestals in the Flower Garden. Within the room there was a central vista out towards an obelisk sited in what was an antechamber now known as TORTE'S GARDEN [2], because the first of our cats, the Lady Torte de Shell, lies buried there. The obelisk has also moved elsewhere and in its place there is a small container filled with sempervivums. This small area is virtually unchanged from when it was planted in September 1974: four Irish yew flanked by conifers – *Chamaecyparis lawsoniana* 'Somerset', *C. l.* 'Wisseli', *C. l.* 'Erecta Viridis' and *C. l.* 'Wyevale Silver', *Cupressus arizonica* var. *glabra* 'Conica', and *Juniperus virginiana* 'Burkii'. A thuja hedge was planted to screen out the dilapidated pond in which, at a later date, I cut a window. The shrubs here are *Mahonia* x *media* 'Charity' and *M. pinnata* and in spring there is an underplanting of daffodils. Behind the hedge is a working area but it is also where the catalpa tree called the Second Lord Plunket grows.

Initially the interior of the Yew Garden consisted of a series of symmetrical beds cut into the turf and planted with box infilled with thyme and santolina, virtually all of which died in the drought of 1976. The following year I planted my first serious small parterre of *Buxus sempervirens* 'Suffruticosa' and two others with our initials in box, R and J. The latter the gardeners almost immediately destroyed with weedkiller and were replaced by two hawthorn standards. Nothing much happened to this garden until 1980, when a large room was added to the house necessitating its replanning. The inherited artificial well was demolished and the concealing hedge of the yew room facing the house was swept away, the sides being extended towards the house. The finials were re-sited and underplanted with rosemary and standard roses were planted in perspective, although all of them were killed in the frost of 1981. It was then that the present *Amelanchier lamarckii* were planted, each inset into a clipped 'Versailles tub' of *Crataegus*. In 1982, on the demise of my father-in-law, the Lion from Barry's Houses of Parliament [a] arrived and was sited in its present position (see above, page 142). After we came to live here the existing parterre was enlarged and a second one of equal size was created in 1990, both to designs by Julia. It was then that they were planted in spring in patterns with orange and white tulips and orange crown imperials. In 1992 the conservatory was built and the existing stone terrace made with its pierced screening, the finials being moved to the Flower Garden. The screening is engulfed with honeysuckle, rosemary and a *Clematis tangutica* and the terrace area and walls around the house planted with *Bergenia cordifolia*, thyme, primroses, a 'Brown Turkey' fig, *Jasminum humile* and *Chaenomeles speciosa* 'Simonii' and *C.* x *superba* 'Jet Trail' and *C.* x *s.* 'Crimson and Gold'. A *Hydrangea anomala* subsp. *petiolaris*

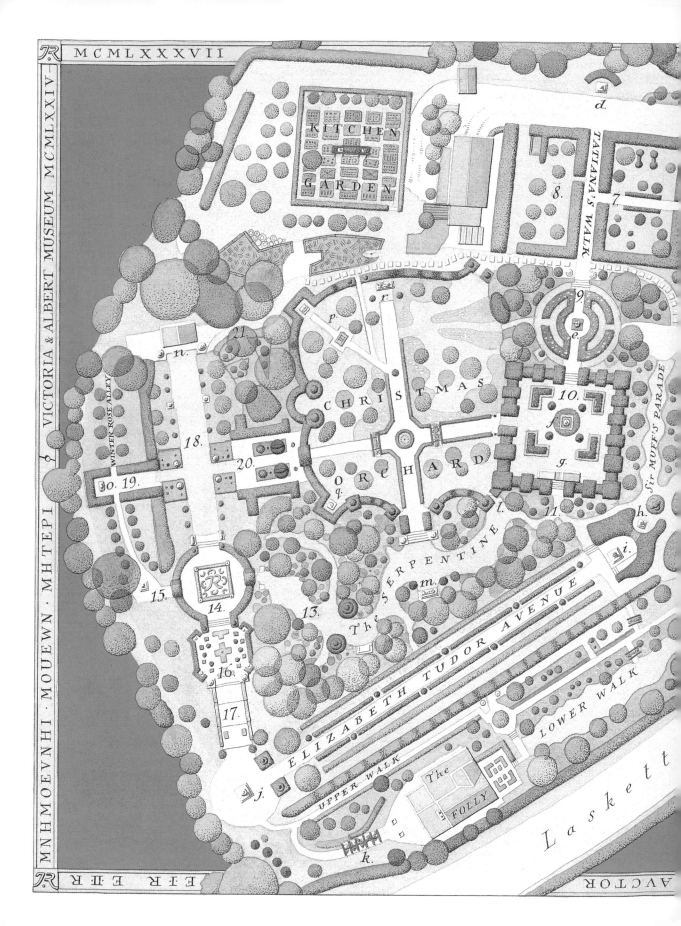

CIRCVMSPICE ♪ HOMO ♪ SVM ♪

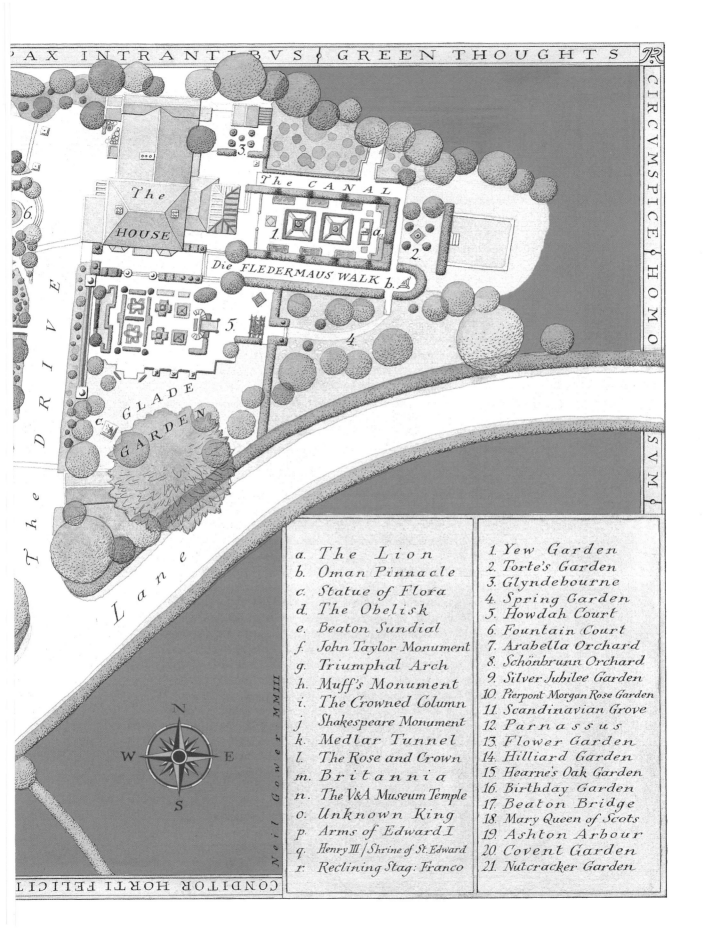

The CANAL

The HOUSE

Die FLEDERMAUS WALK

The DRIVE

GLADE GARDEN

Lane

a. The Lion
b. Oman Pinnacle
c. Statue of Flora
d. The Obelisk
e. Beaton Sundial
f. John Taylor Monument
g. Triumphal Arch
h. Muff's Monument
i. The Crowned Column
j. Shakespeare Monument
k. Medlar Tunnel
l. The Rose and Crown
m. Britannia
n. The V&A Museum Temple
o. Unknown King
p. Arms of Edward I
q. Henry III / Shrine of St. Edward
r. Reclining Stag: Franco

1. Yew Garden
2. Torte's Garden
3. Glyndebourne
4. Spring Garden
5. Howdah Court
6. Fountain Court
7. Arabella Orchard
8. Schönbrunn Orchard
9. Silver Jubilee Garden
10. Pierpont Morgan Rose Garden
11. Scandinavian Grove
12. Parnassus
13. Flower Garden
14. Hilliard Garden
15. Hearne's Oak Garden
16. Birthday Garden
17. Beaton Bridge
18. Mary Queen of Scots
19. Ashton Arbour
20. Covent Garden
21. Nutcracker Garden

Neil Gower MMIII

N W E S

the spandrel beds and, from time to time, a rich planting of tulips in the central one. Reconstituted-stone pineapples flank an exit into the Christmas Orchard. The Rose Garden is really at its height in late June into July, taking over from the Jubilee.

From there the visitor descends to the SCANDINAVIAN GROVE [11], so called after the silver birch trees. These determine the garden's life, for this is a springtime garden which bursts into bloom from early January and is over when the leaves come onto the trees in April. It consists of a small rectangle of land held in, on one side, by the yew hedging of the Rose Garden and, on the other, by clipped laurels. The paths, little more than tracks, lead to Elizabeth Tudor, Sir Muff's Parade and the Serpentine. In the middle is a *Prunus* x *subhirtella* 'Autumnalis Rosea'. The planting is wholly informal, resembling a verdure tapestry of flowers which include: *Helleborus hybridus*, *Helleborus foetidus* varieties, wild garlic, yellow crown imperials, *Pulmonaria* varieties, white and purple violets, primroses, snakeshead fritillaries, a violet *Vinca*, Doronicum, Lamium, *Primula* varieties, *Corydalis flexuosa* 'China Blue', *C. f.* 'Purple Leaf', *C. f.* 'Nightshade' and *C. f.* 'Père David', cowslips, *Viola* 'Coeur d'Alsace', *Asarum europaeum*, *Galanthus* 'Brenda Troyle', *Ajuga reptans* 'Atropurpurea', *Narcissus assoanus*, *Hepatica* x *media* 'Ballardii', *Tellima* and *Narcissus* 'Tête-à-tête'.

Turning left the visitor comes to SIR MUFF'S PARADE, a walk bounded on one side by the yew hedge of the Rose Garden and on the other by a bank running parallel with the drive with a gravel walk along its summit. At the top end is a small PARNASSUS [12], a seat amidst a shrub planting of evergreens including Portugal laurel, common laurel, *Aucuba*, *Osmanthus delavayi*, *Pyracantha* 'Teton'. The seat is encompassed by a blue *treillage* arbour up which climbs *Lonicera periclymenum* 'Graham Thomas' and *Fremontodendron* 'California Glory'. This area incorporates early plantings of conifers, *Thuja occidentalis*, *Chamaecyparis pisifera* 'Plumosa Aurea', *Calocedrus decurrens* and also a *Ginkgo biloba*. There is box hedging and underplanting which includes *Helleborus* varieties, dicentras and ferns. Opposite the Parnassus a short flight of steps leads to the gravel walk along the mount. The walk is punctuated with blue treillage arches up which grow yellow *Rosa* 'Laura Ford' and white *Rosa* 'Félicité Perpétue'. To the eastern side of that mount there is a planting of trees and shrubs: pollarded *Robinia pseudoacacia*, silver birch, *Acer platanoides* 'Drummondii', *Aronia arbutifolia* 'Erecta' and *Cornus kousa* var. *chinensis*. Beneath there is wild planting into the field grass of primroses, cowslips and snowdrops.

From the Parnassus there is a paved area followed by the grass walk called Sir Muff's Parade, which is flanked by crinkle-crankle borders at the foot of a short avenue of pollarded *Robinia pseudoacacia* interplanted on the eastern side with *Malus* 'Butterball', M. 'White

Star', 'Stellata' and *M. spectabilis*, and on the western with *Malus* x *purpurea*, *M.* 'Golden Nugget' and *M. orthocarpa*. On either side the borders are filled with a mixed planting including *Sidalcea* 'Sussex Beauty', *Ribes sanguineum* 'White Icicle', *Lysimachia punctata*, *Helleborus* varieties, *Pulmonaria* 'Mawson's Blue' and *P. rubra* 'Bowles Red', *Astilbe* x *arendsii* 'Brautschleier', *Campanula glomerata* var. *alba*, *Anthemis tinctoria* 'E. C. Buxton', *Actaea* (syn. *Cimicifuga*) *matsumurae* 'White Pearl', *Aucuba japonica* 'Crotonifolia', *Buxus sempervirens*, *Tellima*, *Ligularia dentata* 'Desdemona', *Tiarella* 'Mint Chocolate', *Skimmia* x *confusa* 'Kew Green', *Pieris japonica* 'Debutante', *Ilex aquifolium* 'Silver Lining' and 'Elegantissima', *Thalictrum delavayi* (syn. *T. dipterocarpum*), martagon lilies, *Leucanthemum* x *superbum* 'Sonnenschein', *Physostegia virginiana* 'Rosea', *Astilbe chinensis* var. *pumila*, *Chamaecyparis lawsoniana* 'Golden Wonder', *Campanula punctata* f. *rubriflora* and geranium varieties.

At the far end of Sir Muff's Parade stands the solitary yew from Sutton Place with its topiary crown (see above, page 184) with an underplanting in spring of hyacinths. Behind the yew stands the monument to the Rev. Wenceslas Muff [h] (see above, pages 215–16), from which a gravel path leads through to the avenue ELIZABETH TUDOR. What is seen at present is the third successive avenue, the first being of poplars, the second of *Nothofagus nervosa*, the third and final of pleached *Tilia platyphyllos* 'Rubra'. The limes are trained to form three tiers and underplanted with a swagged beech hedge. Within that is a strip of grass filled in spring with daffodils. The central path is bordered by a low yew hedge punctuated with holly standards and a row of large staggered Irish yew. On the northern side the avenue is backed by a leylandii hedge while, on the southern, the backing is part of the Serpentine shrubbery, a mixture of conifers (including *Thuja plicata*, *Chamaecyparis lawsoniana* 'Lanei Aurea', x *Cupressocyparis leylandii* 'Castlewellan'), silver birch trees, *Taxus baccata*, common laurel, *Pyracantha*, *Viburnum tinus* (laurustinus), *Elaeagnus*, *Viburnum* x *bodnantense* and purple berberis.

At the eastern end there is the CROWNED COLUMN [i] celebrating Elizabeths I and II, with both their crowns and initials on slate plaques on the base pedestal (see above, pages 217–18, 227). This is backed by an exedra of clipped laurel. To the south is a *Malus* x *magdeburgensis*. At the opposite end of the avenue stands the SHAKESPEARE MONUMENT [j] (see above, page 146), framed by two large topiary yews together with clipped Portugal laurels and backed by an exedra of x *Cupressocyparis leylandii* 'Castlewellan' and other evergreen shrubs. In the vicinity there are Malus varieties: *M.* x *robusta* 'Red Siberian', *M.* 'Golden Gem', *M.* x *adstringens* 'Hopa', *M.* x *zumi* 'Golden Hornet' and *M.* x *moerlandsii* 'Liset'.

laxifolia, nepeta, rue, bronze lysimachia, *Phlomis fruticosa* and *Stachys byzantina*. In spring there are hyacinths, 'Woodstock' and 'Splendid Cornelia', followed by *Allium albopilosum* and A. 'Purple Sensation'.

The **VICTORIA & ALBERT MUSEUM TEMPLE** [n] is really the climax of any garden tour with its inscription in Greek, the key to the garden, 'Memory, Mother of the Muses'. Its erection in 1988 I have described above (pages 163–8), but it was built into an existing planting of Dawyck beech and a *Betula pendula* 'Tristis', a present from Angela Conner and John Bulmer, planted in the autumn of 1977. The Temple is flanked by busts of Victoria and Albert silhouetted against blue trellis which is planted with, among other things, *Rosa* 'Paul's Himalayan Musk', *Clematis montana* 'Elizabeth', *Rosa* 'Veilchenblau' and *Vitis coignetiae*.

From the Temple the visitor moves into the **NUTCRACKER GARDEN** [21], named after the production Julia did for the Royal Opera House. This is an informal area around a *Liquidambar* and a *Cedrus atlantica* as well as a large *Prunus lusitanica*. There are more *Malus: M. pumila* 'Cowichan', *M. x atrosanguinea*, *M. hupehensis* (syn. *M. theifera*), *M. x robusta* 'Yellow Siberian', *M. x purpurea* 'Eleyi', *M. x micromalus* (syn. *M.* 'Kaido'), *M. kansuensis*, *M. baccata* 'Lady Northcliffe', *M. x moerlandsii*, *M. pumila* 'Niedzwetzkyana', *M. x robusta*, *M. sylvestris*, *M. transitoria* and 'Veitch's Scarlet'. There are roses, *Rosa* 'Frühlingsgold' and 'Frühlingsmorgen' and *Rosa* 'Wickwar'. In spring there are naturalized bulbs, aconites, snowdrops, *Anemone blanda* and narcissi. Raised beds surrounded by clipped box cones are filled with hellebores, violets, tulips, iris and *Anemone* x *hybrida* 'Elegans'.

From here or via Covent Garden we enter the **CHRISTMAS ORCHARD**. This is now quartered by paths bordered east–west by a low beech hedge and north–south by a low yew hedge flanked by two pairs of fastigiate golden yew to emphasize the perspective to the recumbent stag we call **FRANCO** [r] and on which there is the quotation from Milton's *Paradise Lost* (see above, pages 207, 219). The Orchard is encompassed by a yew hedge cut into swags, pompoms and cake-stands with bays accommodating sculpture, a bust of Diana in reconstituted stone and two original pieces, both from the pre-1834 Palace of Westminster, one medieval, the arms of Edward I [p] (see above, pages 201–202), part of the Thames Embankment facade, and the other early nineteenth century, Henry III holding in one hand a model of the Shrine of St Edward the Confessor in Westminster Abbey [q] (appropriate, for after its acquisition in 1998, I was to become two years later High Bailiff and Searcher of the Sanctuary there). Over the east–west path straddle two arches of carpentry work supporting the rose 'Phyllis

Bide' leading to the Rose Garden, which is prefaced by two small statues of Boy Warriors. The Orchard itself has a floral sequence, beginning in spring with a bouquet of snowdrops beneath the Stag followed by white hyacinths. Then avenues of several varieties of narcissi criss-cross the Orchard, the most important being the flanging planting of 'Sempre Avanti' on either side of the north–south path. Around the arms of Edward I there are blue, white and red (pink, really) hyacinths representing the colours of the Union Jack in reference to the armorial which commemorates the publication of *The Story of Britain*. The spring flowers lead on to the blossom on the fruit trees and then come roses and standard *Wisteria sinensis*. The roses include a number of the Rugosa 'Roseraie de l'Haÿ', *Rosa* 'F. J. Grootendorst', 'Céleste', 'Noisette Carnée', *Rosa roxburghii* and *Rosa rubiginosa* (syn. *R. eglanteria*). In the autumn the roses provide hips, and the fruit follows on the trees.

The fruit trees are all dwarf rooting stock and include the following apples: 'Bramley's Seedling', 'Egremont Russet', 'Kidd's Orange Red', 'Lord Lambourne', 'Sunset', 'Tydeman's Late Orange', 'Warner's King', 'Worcester Pearmain', 'Beauty of Bath', 'Reverend W. Wilks', 'Pitmaston Duchess', 'Rosemary Russet', 'Braddick's Nonpareil', 'Ingrid Marie', 'Mabbott's Pearmain', 'King's Acre Pippin', 'Doctor Harvey', 'Api Rose', 'Keswick Codling', 'Norfolk Beefing', 'Catshead', 'Costard', 'Herefordshire Beefing', 'Yellow Ingestre', 'Calville Blanc d'Hiver', 'King's Acre Bountiful', 'Brabant Bellefleur', 'Scotch Bridget', 'Bess Pool', 'Kentish Fillbasket', 'Lady Sudeley' and 'Lord Hindlip'. Pears include 'Joséphine de Malines', 'Doyenné du Comice', 'Vicar of Winkfield', 'Pitmaston Duchess', 'Winter Nelis', 'Packham's Triumph', 'Beurré Superfin' and 'Beurré Hardy'. There is also a 'Prune Damson' (syn. 'Shropshire Prune') and a quince.

Leaving the Orchard the path leads to the KITCHEN GARDEN. Within this practical working area there is a small greenhouse, compost heaps, a space for a bonfire, sheds for storing tools and equipment, beds for cuttings and dumps. The Kitchen Garden is a practical space the size of one and a half tennis courts with one decorative element, a series of wooden arches which form a central vertical feature, up which climbs the 'Gardener's Rose' and honeysuckle. The beds are all raised and accommodate a rotation of crops designed to keep the house in vegetables and salad greens for as much of the year as possible. Herbs are also accommodated here. Around the enclosure are fruit bushes and also more fruit trees, including plums: 'Pershore' (syn. 'Yellow Egg'), 'Marjorie's Seedling', 'Aylesbury Prune' damson, 'Laxton Cropper', 'Victoria' and 'Warwickshire Drooper'; apples: 'Lane's Prince Albert', 'Charles Ross', 'Annie Elizabeth', 'Cox's Orange Pippin', 'Queen

Cox', 'Peasgood's Nonsuch', 'Newton Wonder', 'Howgate Wonder', 'Blenheim Orange', 'Orleans Reinette' and 'Laxton's Superb', and pears: 'Louise Bonne of Jersey' and 'Glou Morceau'.

The path out of the Kitchen Garden leads down to the house past a group of medlars and the exedra framing an OBELISK [d] which forms the close of the great vista from the Rose Garden. The visitor finds himself back in the Fountain Court having covered the whole garden.

Marketplace: ebyuk_brit
Order Number: 10663390
Customer Name: Sam Gardener
Order Date: 27/11/2022
Marketplace Order #: 02-09398-64543
Currency: GBP

Locator
BOC-1-M-5-5-3151

	Condition	**Price**
	Used; Good	3.53

Subtotal:	3.53
Shipping:	0.00
Total:	3.53

r your order!
order, please contact us at customercare@britbooks.co.uk

P
MK11
customer

Qty	Item
1	The Laskett
	Strong, Roy
	SKU: 910,318

Notes:

If you have any questions or concerns regard

PHOTOGRAPH CREDITS

The copyright in the photographs on pages 18, 19, 30, 31, 35, 36, 37, 38, 40, 41, 46, 47, 66, 67, 68, 69, 70, 71, 74, 75, 76, 77, 89, 91, 92, 93, 94, 95, 99, 102, 103, 120, 121, 127, 128, 129, 139, 144, 152, 154, 155, 156, 163, 169, 178, 179, 180, 183, 190, 191, 192, 212, 213, 214, 215, 217, 229, and 249 is the property of Oman Productions Limited. The rights of Oman Productions Limited to be identified as the author of the photographs have been asserted in accordance with ss.77and 78 of the Copyright, Designs and Patents Act 1988.

2, 10/11, 34, 79, 82/3, 96/7, 98 (top), 105, 131, 132/3, 137, 158/9, 176/7, 203, 207, 216, 227, 231, 232/3, 238/9, 242/3, 248: Andrew Lawson; 9, 26/7, 50/1, 72/3, 100/01, 110, 118/19, 138, 140/41, 143, 147, 150/51, 161, 164/5, 167, 168, 172, 186/7, 194/5, 204/5, 220, 224/5, 228: Gary Rogers, Hamburg; 13: courtesy Michael Leonard; 15: Cecil Beaton by courtesy of Sotheby's London; 42, 44/5, 209: Anthony Kersting; 56/7: Country Life Picture Library; 59, 60, 62: Georgina Masson/American Academy in Rome; 87, 160: Jerry Harpur; 104, 106: Tony Lord; 113, 196: Clive Boursnell/Country Life Picture Library; 149: Edwin Smith/British Architectural Library, RIBA, London; 210: Alex Ramsay/Country Life Picture Library; 247: Charlie Hopkinson. The endpapers are by Jonathan Myles-Lea.

The remaining images are from the author's collection. Every effort has been made to trace copyright holders and any who have not been contacted are invited to get in touch with the publishers.

ACKNOWLEDGEMENTS

INSPIRED EDITORS ARE RARE IN AN AUTHOR'S CAREER. FRANCESCA LIVERSIDGE IS ONE such, and her commitment to this book, and also that of her colleagues at Bantam, has been total. I can't thank them enough for sharing a vision. In particular I'd like to mention Sheila Lee, who worked tirelessly on the illustrations, and Mari Roberts, who not only copyedited the book but also orchestrated its smooth way through the press. Kenneth Carroll had the design ideas, which were beautifully brought to fruition by Julia Lloyd. I'm grateful to Tony Lord for his horticultural expertise, exercised in these pages, and I'd also like to thank Neil Gower for his thrilling new aerial view of The Laskett garden. To these I must add my literary agent, Felicity Bryan, whose encouragement during the initial stages was crucial. Lastly I must mention my wife, whose book it is as much as mine, and whose passion for snapping the transient moment has enriched these pages so signally.

ROY STRONG

A SPRING & A TEMPLE

KITCHEN GARDEN

COMPOST

The Cathedral

TATIANA'S WALK

10

11

FRANCO

LUCIA

CHRISTMAS ORCHARD

12

WINTER ROSE WALK

MARY QUEEN OF SCOTS WALK

ENGLAND ALLEY

22

21

23

20

19

18

14

FLOWER GARDEN SERPENTINE

15

16

13

ELIZABETH TUDOR AVENUE

WINTER

HILLIARD GARDEN

The Folly

17

TO LLANWARNE

Jonathan